Big Fat Cat
vs.
MR. JONES

Takahiko Mukoyama
Tetsuo Takashima
with studio ET CETERA

윌북

• 영어를 이해하는 데 굳이 번역문은 필요하지 않다는 저자의 뜻에 따라 우리말 해석을 싣지 않았습니다. 하지만 이 책을 다 본 후에 정확한 번역을 확인하고 싶다면 윌북 영어 카페에 들러주세요. 언제든 환영합니다.
cafe.naver.com/everville

PREVIOUSLY IN THE BIG FAT CAT SERIES

지금까지의 **BIG FAT CAT** 시리즈

Big Fat Cat
and
The MUSTARD PIE

FORMER BIG CITY BUSINESSMAN, ED WISHBONE IS NOW A BAKER IN A SMALL TOWN.

THAT CAT STOLE THE PIE AGAIN!

HIS USUAL DAY BEGINS WITH A BATTLE WITH HIS PET CAT.

A BATTLE THAT HE ALWAYS LOSES.

BUT OTHERWISE... HIS LIFE IS SIMPLE AND PEACEFUL.

AT LEAST IT WAS... UNTIL TODAY.

YOUR SHOP WAS SOLD.

SUDDENLY AND UNEXPECTEDLY...

...ED'S LIFE BEGAN TO FALL APART.

ED TRIED TO SAVE HIS SHOP BUT FAILED.

BADLY.

CAATT!

CRUMBLE!

HIS SHOP AND HOME WERE QUICKLY TORN DOWN.

ED WISHBONE'S LONG JOURNEY HAD BEGUN.

4

LATER THAT DAY, ED SET OUT TO TOWN.

Big Fat Cat GOES TO TOWN

HIS FIRST STOP :

VACANCY IN FOOD COURT

THE NEW MALL.

A SIGN ADVERTISED A VACANT SPOT IN THE FOOD COURT OF THE NEW MALL.

JEREMY JR., THE SON OF A LOCAL MILLIONARE WAS ALREADY THERE FOR THE SPOT, BUT THE OWNER GAVE ED A CHANCE. ---"PAY ONE MONTH'S RENT BEFORE CLOSING TIME AND THE SHOP IS YOURS."

THE TIME LIMIT WAS ONE HOUR.

TICK

Hook you with Pan P

Neverland P

TICK
TICK
TICK

OWNER OF THE MALL

JEREMY LIGHT-FOOT JR.

BILLY BOB

ED RAN TO THE BANK AND MADE IT BACK...

CAT! STOP...

BUT ANOTHER BAD LUCK STRUCK HIM.

sssKKRREEE

AND NOW, HE HAD LOST EVERYTHING...

...ALMOST MADE IT BACK.

...EVEN HIS CAT.

5

Big Fat Cat AND THE GHOST AVENUE

A COLD WINTER NIGHT.

ED WISHBONE IS ALONE, SEARCHING FOR HIS CAT.

HE FALLS ASLEEP IN AN OLD DESERTED GHOST STREET UPTOWN.

AND IS AWAKENED BY 'GHOSTS.'

WOOOOOo

THE 'GHOSTS' OF GHOST AVENUE.

PEOPLE FORGOTTEN FROM THE REAL WORLD.

PEOPLE WHO HAVE NOT HAD A SLICE OF PIE IN MANY YEARS.

PEOPLE WITH LIVES MUCH WORSE THAN ED COULD EVER IMAGINE.

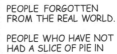

ED WISHBONE LEARNED A LESSON THAT WINTER NIGHT.

THANK YOU.

LIFE IS NOT A SWEET PIE.

SOMETIMES, IT'S UNFAIR.

BUT OTHER TIMES, IT'S FAIR...

AND YOU JUST HAVE TO EAT THE PIE YOU GET.

HA HA HA!

SEASON 1 THE END

SO EAT IT.

ONE MONTH LATER.

ED IS BACK INTO BUSINESS WITH HIS NEW FRIENDS AND NEW CUSTOMERS...

Big Fat Cat AND THE MAGIC PIE SHOP

A LOT OF NEW CUSTOMERS.

SOME PEOPLE ARE NOT AMUSED WITH THIS.

JEREMY SR. IS ONE OF THEM. HE DOES NOT LIKE ATTENTION FOCUSED ON GHOST AVENUE.

PIES.

SHROOOOK

THEY WIN THE FIGHT, BUT PAY A BIG PRICE IN RETURN: OLD WILLY SUFFERS A HEART ATTACK.

JEREMY JR. COMES TO INVADE THE SHOP AND ED AND THE GHOSTS FIGHT BACK WITH THEIR ONLY WEAPON.

THINGS LOOK BAD.

WILLY NEEDS A DOCTOR BADLY.

BUT DOCTORS COST MONEY.

AND MONEY IS SOMETHING THEY DON'T HAVE.

$20,000

IT'S TIME FOR THE PIEGAMES.

NEXT ISSUE:
BIG FAT CAT
VS.
MR.JONES

"George..."

"George..."

"It's morning."

"Oh... Ed. Good morning," George said. He rubbed his <ruby>비비다</ruby> sleepy eye with one hand as he got up.

The sun was barely up in the sky. Fresh and crisp air filled the dawn of Everville's older streets. It was seven o'clock in the morning —— the beginning of a new day.

After a moment of <ruby>회복</ruby> recovery, George smiled and pointed before him.

"There's your <ruby>물건</ruby> stuff. Good and ready."

In front of George, there was a pile of kitchen utensils that
Ed used everyday. They were the cheapest brand at the nearby
supermarket, but now they shined like silver in the morning light.
Ed noticed that George's hands were all red.

"This was all I could do. But I'll be in the front row today,
cheering like hell," George said.

Ed picked up his rolling pin. Yesterday, it had been an old
gray color. Now it was practically new.

"George... we don't have any sandpaper. This is impossible.
How did you..."

George took out a completely worn-out toothbrush. He
grinned like a child.

Ed stood amazed. He couldn't imagine how many hours it
would take to scrub a rolling pin with a toothbrush.

"George, this is impossible!"

"Almost," George said and smiled.

Ed touched the rolling pin with the tip^끝 of his fingers. He thought he could feel the warmth inside.

"George, you can't sit in the front row today," he said to George.

"Oh..."

A look of despair^절망 crossed George's face for a moment. But he replied quickly. He was used to^익숙해져 있다 this kind of^종류 treatment^대우 all his life.

"Oh... well, I know. I guess I would make a bad impression^인상 on the judges. Hey, no problem! I'll just stay in the back and keep..."

Ed held the contest flier out to George. An entry form and a list of rules were printed on the back. Ed pointed to one particular^특정한 rule.

"It says here, I can bring one assistant." Ed smiled. "You're going to be that assistant."

"Say what?" George replied. His face turned red as he looked up at Ed. He immediately shook his head.

"No way, man. You don't want me! Uh-un! I'll just mess things up. I always do."

"I went to the Mall yesterday and registered. You already are my assistant, George. I need your help," Ed said.

George stared at Ed.

The morning sun, now higher in the sky, gave bright light onto the old neighborhood. Most of the others were still asleep and the street was quiet.

"Are you sure?" George asked.

Ed nodded.

"Nobody ever asked for my help. Ed... you're... you're so..." George said in a trembling voice.

"Come on, George," Ed said, looking up into the blue sky. It seemed to be the start of a really nice winter day. "Let's get going."

"*You're damn right, we're going!*" George shouted as he stood up in pride.

And with that, the day began.

"AAAAND IT'S A GREAT NEW DAY!! The balloons are up! We're on top of the New Everville Mall this morning, reporting live from the annual State Pie Festival! This is Glen Hamperton, bringing you the excitement below —live on the morning news!"

BFC BOOKS PART FIVE

Big Fat Cat
vs.
MR. JONES

Today, eighteen shops and individuals enter the pie contest
to find the best pie in the state. This year's main sponsor Wilson
Artwill, the owner of the New Everville Mall, has prepared a
huge cash prize of twenty thousand dollars and a free space for a
shop in his Food Court.

The rules are simple. Contestants have two hours to bake
the best pie. They can use any ingredients they choose, but each
contestant can have only one assistant for help.

At the end of two hours, all the pies will be presented to the judges. Each contestant will introduce their pie in the way they wish. After tasting all eighteen pies, the judges will each vote for the best pie. The numbers will be added up, and the single contestant with the highest score will win the 'GOLDEN CRUST' trophy along with the prize money and the store space! The excitement is heating up as the time draws near for the battle of the pies to begin!

"WELCOME TO THE PIEGAMES!"

"I'm Glen Hamperton reporting live from the air above Everville! See you later, folks!"

The street was still quiet.

It was nearly nine a.m., but in Ghost Avenue, morning was longer than any other place. Ed crept through the piles of junk inside the Old Everville Cinema, heading towards the campfire in the middle. BeeJees was half-asleep near the fire. Besides him, Willy lay on a fake bed that Ed and the others had made.

Willy hadn't woken up once in two days. He was still alive, but barely.

"Willy," Ed whispered.

But Willy didn't react.

"I have to go. But I'll be back soon. Then we'll get you to a hospital, okay?" Ed said.

The light of the fire fell on Willy's face. Sometimes the flickering light made Willy seem to move a little. Unfortunately, it was always only a trick of the eye.

A faint cracking sound broke the silence. Ed looked behind
him and found BeeJees awake, slumped against an old sign.
BeeJees was holding a fortune cookie which he had just cracked
open in his hands.

"BeeJees, I'm sorry about what I said the other night," Ed said
to BeeJees. "I... I'm really sorry."

BeeJees scratched his head, frowned, and looked down. He
pulled out a thin piece of paper from inside the fortune cookie.
After a long pause, he read from the paper in a flat voice.

"There are chances, and there are consequences."

BeeJees shook his head and chuckled. "What the hell does
that mean?"

He dropped the paper and cookie on the floor and crushed^{눌러 부수다} them under his foot.

"The Prof loved these things. The Chinese store downtown used to give him cookies that had expired.^{기한이 끝나다} He cracked one open every morning and read the paper inside. It always said something stupid^{어리석은} like that. He just read them and smiled. That crazy old bastard.^{못된 인간}"

BeeJees laughed weakly.

Ed had taken his bandanna out and was folding^{접다} it in half. He wrapped it around his head and tied it in the back. Right then, Frank came rolling around the corner in his toy wagon. He said "Howdy" to Ed and waved at him. Ed waved back.

"You really think you can win this contest?" BeeJees asked.

Ed held a solemn^{심각한} expression^{표정} on his face, but his eyes were determined.^{결연한} BeeJees cracked open another fortune cookie. This time, he crushed it without even reading the paper inside.

"Do you at least have a plan? Everyone else in the contest is a professional.^{프로} You're just a guy^{사람} from a small town. What do you plan to do?"

"What Willy told me." Ed reached for his bag as he said, "Try to be a baker."

Ed started for the door, looking back at Willy one last time.
Willy slept on, cuddled in a pile of dirty rags.

At least he deserves a better bed, Ed thought. It made him want
to cry. But there was no time for crying.

"Watch the cat for me, Frank. It's going to be a disaster if the
cat finds out where I'm going," Ed said to Frank.

"Ai-ya!" Frank replied.

George was waiting by the doors, dressed in his best outfit. It
was a cheap tuxedo. He looked like a boy waiting for his first day
of Sunday school. This made Ed smile again.

"Ed," BeeJees suddenly shouted. Ed looked back as BeeJees
threw him a fortune cookie. Ed caught the cookie with both
hands.

"Take Willy with you," BeeJees said.

Ed raised his eyes and nodded once.

It was time to go.

"This is Glen Hamperton, reporting from outside the main tent of the State Pie Festival. The time is now ten a.m. and contestants should be here any minute now... and YES! Here they come! This year's pie warriors!

"Leading the group is the two-time contest winner 'Brown Butters' — now at four locations around the state. Their famous 'Brown Butter Vanilla Double Crust' has been the number one best-selling pie for more than fifteen years!

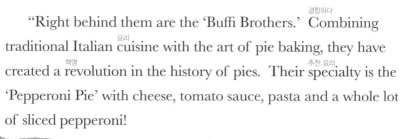

"Right behind them are the 'Buffi Brothers.' Combining
traditional Italian cuisine with the art of pie baking, they have
created a revolution in the history of pies. Their specialty is the
'Pepperoni Pie' with cheese, tomato sauce, pasta and a whole lot
of sliced pepperoni!

결합하다

요리

혁명

추천 요리

"And... oh my God... what is that blue smoke back there!?
Has there been an accident? No, wait... that music, that rhythm...
Yes, everyone! This is the one you've been waiting for! The
crowd is going crazy! We now present you, the one and only...
ZOMBIE PIES!!

"It's the strangest pie shop in the history of strange pie shops! The Pie God himself, Jeremy Lightfoot Jr., and the colorful Zombie Pies trailer are now entering the tent. Their horrifying mascot, 'The Gravedigger,' stalks the grounds while the 'Grim Zombies' are scaring kids who unfortunately got in their way! Already condemned by twenty-one school boards, Zombie Pies is nevertheless the most famous pie shop in ten surrounding states!

♪ WE'RE NOT YOUR MOTHER'S APPLE PIES! ♪

Banned from 2122 school boards!

"Reporting live from the entrance of the PIEGAMES, I'm Glen Hamperton! The battle is about to begin!!"

Meanwhile... at the main gate.

"Oh my God..." George said, and forgot to shut his mouth.
"Ed, I think this is a big mistake."

George stared at the fabulous Zombie Pies trailer truck as it
entered the tent, his mouth wide open.

Ed was also frozen there at the gate of the pie festival. He
scanned the festival grounds with both his eyes, surprised at how
big the event was. There was a Ferris wheel standing at the far
side, along with several other carnival rides.

셀 수 없이 많은
Countless booths selling every kind of pie on earth were
lined back to back down the main area. People of all ages were
everywhere. There were balloons, flags, and other multi-colored
장식
decorations all around.

Before arriving at the festival grounds, Ed had imagined an
강당
auditorium with fifty or a hundred people. He couldn't have been
more wrong.
침을 꿀꺽 삼키다
Ed gulped.

George looked at Ed with big, frightened-puppy eyes. George was probably the only person in the whole festival grounds wearing a tuxedo, except for the stuffed bear on the counter of a nearby booth.

"This is crazy, man. BeeJees is right. We're waaaay out of our league here. Let's go home."

George turned to leave, but Ed grabbed his arm.

"George, we've got no choice."

"I know, man. But I'm scared."

"Me too," Ed said, and started walking towards the main tent. George stood there alone at the gate for a moment. But when people nearby began to look at him suspiciously, he started to run after Ed — but fell because of his shaking legs. He got up and continued to run.

"Ed! Hey! Wait up! Ed!"

Unnoticed by either of them, a dark shadow crouched by the gate silently, watching everything.

"Thank you, Glen. And now, this is your host Robert R. Silverman from inside the main tent. Almost all of the contestants have finished setting up their kitchens here on the battleground. All we can do is wait for the clock to... oops, someone just came into the tent from the contestant's side."

"Hey, mister, you've got the wrong gate! But, oh... wait a minute... am I dreaming this, or... Good Lord! This man seems to be our last contestant!"

"He has now stopped at booth five. Let's see... his name seems to be 'Ed Wishbone.' Funny, the name sort of rings a bell. Where have I heard... Holy cow! It's the baker from Ghost Avenue! We've all seen him on the six o'clock news! My God, I don't want to be rude here, but Ed, man, maybe you should open your eyes and take a look around!"

재미있는
※
※ (의미 없는 놀람)
무례한

"Uh-oh... More bad news. I'm afraid Mr. Tuxedo here is Ed's
assistant. I just hope that barrel he's dragging isn't what I think it
질질 끌다
is. If this is a joke, it sure seems to work, because everyone in the
stands is laughing like crazy. Ladies and gentlemen, let's just hope
무사한
that the judges' health is still intact when they go home tonight!"

※ (의미 없는 놀람)

"Holy macaroni! Is that his oven!?" Jeremy's assistant said. He was laughing and pointing at Ed as they set up the barrel oven.

George was so embarrassed that he lost his grip, and the barrel oven toppled over. The crowd went wild. Ed and George just kept on trying to balance the barrel. The crowd laughed as if they were watching a circus.

"Is he really going to enter the contest!? Man, talk about crazy people..."

"Shut up," Jeremy said. He was concentrating on checking the oven.

"But boss, you should take a look at this guy. He is totally out of his..."

Jeremy hit the top of the oven hard with his hand. The
assistant stopped babbling. Jeremy was dressed in costume, but
his face was dead serious. He slowly pulled his hand back and hid
it behind him. It hurt.

"I said... quiet. Stop laughing, and keep your mind on your
job."

The surprised assistant replied, "Yes, sir." He got back to
work in a hurry.

Jeremy glanced at Ed and George with a look of disgust, then
focused again on his oven. He tried to dismiss the duo from his
mind, but kept remembering the taste of that pie.

An ordinary pie. *That was all.* An ordinary fruit pie. But he
still couldn't forget the taste. It made him nervous.

"Okay, Wishbone. You're here," Jeremy mumbled. "Now,
prove yourself."

Meanwhile behind the Zombie Pies trailer.

Billy Bob listened to his cell phone in silence. He didn't say anything. He didn't even nod. He just listened. Finally, before hanging up, he said one phrase.

"Yes, sir."

Billy Bob was standing between the trailer and the back wall where almost nobody could see him. He carefully set Mr. Jones' carrier cage down on the ground and moved away into the back alley.

A moment later, Jeremy's assistant came rushing out of the trailer. Jeremy was yelling, "Go get it and hurry!" from behind him. The assistant was so upset that he swung open the back door with all of his might. The door hit Mr. Jones' cage and knocked it over.

The carrier rolled over twice and the door of the cage sprang^{갑자기 튀어오르다}
wide open.

Everything lay still for a while. But then, inch by inch, Mr.
Jones pushed its head out and looked around. ─After a brief^{잠깐 동안의}
pause, Mr. Jones hid inside the cage again.

Another minute passed. Mr. Jones decided to take a step
outside again. It slowly crept out of the cage, and even more
slowly, took one step, then two steps out on the ground.

It felt good. Mr. Jones took a big stretch^{기지개} and narrowed^{좁히다} its
eyes. It then walked over to a trailer tire, sniffed^{냄새 맡다} it, and rubbed a
side against it. Satisfied^{만족하다}, Mr. Jones continued walking down the
alley.

It couldn't understand what was happening, but being outside
of the cage was much better than being inside of it. Free space to
walk around was luxurious^{아주 기분좋은}.

So this was the world outside. The world beyond the bars.^{~을 넘어서   빗장}

34

It was so free, and...

...and it was also pretty scary.

The last time George had seen a real Santa Claus was more than thirty years ago, back in elementary^(초등학교) school. His mom had taken all the kids to the Outside Mall one afternoon, where Santa came every winter. Back then, the Outside Mall was the coolest^(가장 멋진) place a kid could go.

Now, thirty years later, a chubby^(통통한) Santa with a white beard and red suit was walking straight towards them.

"Ed Wishbone?" Santa Claus asked.

George turned to Ed, his eyes wide open.

"You're friends with Santa?" George asked.

Ed looked up from the table as Santa took off his beard. It was the owner of the New Mall.

"Ed Wishbone! I thought that was you!" the owner said. "I was worried after you disappeared from the clinic. Are you okay?"

Ed smiled awkwardly as he replied.

    어색하게

"I'm fine, sir. I'm sorry for everything. I don't really remember much about that night."

"No problem, no problem," the owner said, but the smile faded from his face. "You know, Jeremy Lightfoot's bodyguard came to my office several days after you disappeared. He had a paper with your signature on it. It said that you disclaimed all rights to the space in the Food Court. I knew the paper was suspicious, but I really had no choice but to believe it."

Ed nodded.

"So I didn't rent the space to Zombie Pies, either. Instead, I saved it as the prize for the contest today. I sincerely hope you win."

"Thank you."

"I'm sorry about what happened."

"No. Don't be. It was all for the best. I..."

Just then, a bell rang throughout the main tent, signaling the start of the contest in five minutes. The owner hurriedly put his beard back on. He smiled at Ed.

"Good luck, Mr. Wishbone."

"Thank you, sir," Ed said.

The owner ran off, his fluffy cap flip-flopping with every step.

"I didn't know Santa's beard was fake," George said in an astonished face.

Ed chuckled and turned back to his table. Everything was ready and in place. The only thing now was to decide what kind of pie to make.

    Ed knelt down and inspected the bags he had brought. In one bag were the ingredients for a blueberry pie. But the other bag held the ingredients for another kind of pie. Ed had not mentioned this to George.

    The safe choice was blueberry. There was no doubt about it. Yet, something inside Ed kept telling him that he should enter the contest with his own pie. Not a pie borrowed from his mother's recipe book.

    But that was risky. It was more than a risk. Yet...

    His hand was moving slowly towards the second bag when George said,

    "Damn! Willy sure would have wanted to see this!"

Ed's hand stopped a few inches from the bag.

He clenched the hand into a fist, then grabbed the bag with
the blueberries in it instead.

Willy. Ed thought to himself. *Think about Willy. You have to
win. No matter what.*

Moments later, the bell rang again, and all of the contestants
sprang to a start. The clock tower standing in the middle of the
tent turned twelve. The host was shouting in excitement. The
crowd roared.

And from there on, everything became a blur. The world
seemed to move in fast-forward.

The battle had begun.

An hour later, Jeremy was about to finish his crust when he noticed Billy Bob standing near Ed Wishbone's booth. Only Jeremy and a few others could have possibly spotted him. He was standing in a shadowy corner.

A bad feeling ran through Jeremy's mind as his busy hands stopped moving for a moment.

Billy Bob was checking to see if Ed Wishbone and his assistant were away from their table. —They were. Ed and George were over by the barrel oven, trying to build up a steady fire.

Before Jeremy could even think, Billy Bob stepped out. He took something from the table and replaced it with something else. It was impossible to determine what it was, but he had definitely done something to Wishbone's materials.

When Ed returned to his table a few seconds later, Billy Bob
had disappeared completely, as if he had never been there.

Jeremy took off his apron and laid it on the table. He hurried
out of the trailer and went racing through the back door. Billy
Bob was just coming down the alley. Enraged, Jeremy confronted
Billy Bob head-on.

"You! What were you doing? Tell me!"

Jeremy grabbed Billy Bob by his jacket and pulled, but Billy
Bob didn't move an inch. Nor did his expression change.

"Did my father tell you to do this?"

Billy Bob didn't answer.

"Damn it! I'm not going to let you and my father mess this up! I'm going to win this on my own!"

Billy Bob's cell phone rang. With one movement, Billy Bob brushed Jeremy aside and pulled his phone out. Jeremy went sprawling to the ground, hitting his elbow hard. Ignoring Jeremy, Billy Bob answered the phone. Only Billy Bob's eyes kept watching Jeremy, as if Jeremy too was a pet.

"It's done," Billy Bob said into the phone, then hung up. He walked away without any more words.

Jeremy closed his eyes in both anger and bitterness. Back in the main arena, the host continued to feed the crowd's excitement. Upbeat music rocked the thin walls. The noise all blended together, erasing all sound, including the voice of Jeremy crying.

"The clock now reads one-forty-five. Only fifteen minutes left!

"Most of the pies are already in the oven. There's a nice smell of sugar and spice in the air as I speak!

"Zombie Pies owner Jeremy Lightfoot Jr. disappeared mysteriously from his kitchen around the end of the first hour. We have no information regarding Lightfoot's disappearance, but it may be part of some secret plan.

"Meanwhile, Ed Wishbone and his assistant, now known to the audience as 'the Tux', have continued to hold the crowd's attention with their very unusual oven.

"Oops, it seems for the moment, Ed has disappeared too. But I think it's a safe guess that this has nothing to do with any secret plan."

NOTICE
NO
SMOKING

MEN

"Wishbone!"

Ed stopped in the middle of the back alley when he heard his name. Jeremy had appeared out of the shadows behind him.

In this damp, dark corridor, all the music and excitement
습기 찬
seemed far away, as if it came from a different world.

Jeremy was alone. He slowly took a few steps towards Ed. Ed
겁먹은 듯이
nervously took a step back.

Jeremy Lightfoot Jr. wore a solemn face. He closed his eyes for a moment, clenched his fists, and just stood there. He seemed like he was fighting something inside of himself.

"I... uh... have to go," Ed said, and took a step back towards his booth as Jeremy opened his mouth.

"Check your pie," Jeremy said.

"What?" Ed asked.

"Your pie. I saw someone mess with your supplies when you weren't looking."

Ed stared at Jeremy.

In the quiet refuge of the back alley, the two young bakers really saw each other for the first time. And for some reason, it seemed like looking into a mirror. They both realized it was not a matter of money or pride or proving anything anymore. It was just about pies now.

"My pie?" Ed whispered, his face clouding.

Jeremy nodded.

Ed glanced at the clock on the wall. There were only thirteen more minutes until time was up. If something was wrong with the pie he was baking now, there was no time to start over again.

"Go," Jeremy said.

Ed nodded. He started to run back but paused briefly only to say to Jeremy,
일순간 멈추다   잠깐 동안

"Thanks."

Jeremy closed his eyes again as Ed went dashing for the door. He couldn't tell Ed who had messed with his stuff, and it hurt.

It hurt very badly.

Ghost Avenue. Same time.

Frank hurled piles of rotting magazines and pieces of wood
<small>내던지다</small> <small>썩어가는</small>
into the fire, trying to warm up the theater. But it was still cold.

The cruel coldness sneaked in through the hole in the roof, the
<small>잔인한</small> <small>살금살금 들어오다</small>
cracks in the wall, the broken windows, and anywhere else it
could.

Willy had started shaking a few minutes ago. BeeJees brought
every rag he could find and wrapped them around Willy but the
shaking didn't subside.
<small>가라앉다</small>

"Frank! More fire! Burn everything! Anything!" BeeJees
shouted frantically.
<small>미친 듯이</small>

Frank immediately took off his jacket and threw it into the
fire. But it was no use.

"Prof! Prof! Hang on! Stay with me, Prof! That kid will be back soon with the money! I know he will! Just hold on!"

Willy kept shaking. BeeJees, tears in his eyes, hugged^{껴안다} Willy from top of the blankets, trying to keep him from falling off the bed. BeeJees was scared. He was so scared.

"Hurry, Ed!" BeeJees said. It sounded like a prayer^{기도}. "Please hurry... Please..."

"George! The oven! Check the pies!"

George looked towards the back door. He saw Ed come running back with a hint of panic in his eyes.

The pies would be done in maybe another five minutes. He couldn't understand why Ed was in such a rush.

"Hey, man. Take it easy. Everything's fine, man."

Ed ran past George, grabbed the mitten hanging on the side of the oven, and without any hesitation, opened the oven door. A cloud of smoke rose out of the small door, making Ed and George cough. Ed knew immediately that something was terribly wrong. There shouldn't be this much smoke inside the oven. He gulped as the smoke began to clear.

As soon as he could see inside, Ed pulled a slightly burned pie out of the oven and hurried over to the table.

"Ed! What the hell are you doing!?" George shouted when he saw Ed take out a cutting knife. "That pie isn't finished yet!"

But Ed cut the pie in half. He broke off a piece of crust, 살짝 담그다 살짝 묻혀보다 dipped it in the filling, and popped it in his mouth. He tasted it for a moment and froze.

Ed said something but the 박수 applause of the audience was getting louder and George couldn't hear him.

"...other pie," Ed said again to George, but most of it was 잠기다 drowned out by the sound of the audience.

"Say what?" George asked close to Ed's ear.

"Get the other pie out of the oven! Fast!" Ed repeated, much louder this time.

Hearing the urgency in Ed's voice, George flew over to the oven and returned quickly with the other pie. Ed cut this one in half too, and tasted a piece of it. His reaction was almost the same. But this time, his face lost color completely.

George also took a piece of the pie and bit into it. Almost instantly, he spit it out.

"God! What the hell...?"

George turned to Ed.

"Someone did something to my stuff," Ed said.

George couldn't understand what Ed said for a moment. Then, the full horror sank in. The pies were ruined. There was no more time left.

Ed glanced at the clock tower.

Seven minutes.

The contest was in full swing. Most of the contestants were carrying finished pies from their booths to the judges' area. Ed could do nothing except stare at the two ruined pies on the table.

"Ed!" George tugged on Ed's sleeve. "C'mon, Ed! We still have time! I'll run and get anything! Just tell me what you need!"

Ed still hadn't recovered control, but he said to George in a trembling voice.

"Heat... two more cups of blueberry in a saucepan."

"Gotcha!"

George dashed away, confident that Ed knew a way to repair the pie. But he didn't. He had started scraping the filling out of the crust, but he knew it was impossible.

There was no way to make a pie in seven minutes.

TO BE CONTINUED

BFC BOOKS PRESENTS:
잃어버린 영역을 찾아서

'번역'이라는 애매모호하고 신비한 세계.
그 문을 열면 이제까지 보지 못했던 새로운 세계가 다가옵니다.
미지의 영역으로, 자, 출발!

'잃어버린 영역'

현재 중학교, 고등학교 및 대학의 영어 교육은 기본적으로 '영어 문장의 번역'에 중심을 두고 있습니다. '영어로는 이해가 되지 않는다 → 그럼 우선 우리말로 바꿔보자'라는 발상이 밑바탕에 깔려 있지요. 영어 교육 현장에서 '영단어를 10개 암기한다'는 것은 '영단어 10개의 우리말 번역을 암기한다'는 것입니다. 이는 영단어 10개를 그 자체로 암기하는 것과는 다소 차이가 있습니다.

우리나라의 영어 교육 방식에 익숙해지면 번역해서 암기하는 것이 외국어를 배우는 유일한 방법이라고 생각하기 쉽지만, 결코 그렇지 않습니다. 효율적인 방법 중의 하나란 사실은 분명하지만, 이 방법은 우선 우리말을 마스터했다는 전제 조건이 충족되어야 합니다. 우리말이 서투른 사람이나 아직 어린 아이들에게는 불가능한 방법이지요. 그리고 이 학습법에는 치명적인 약점이 있습니다.

'번역'이 100퍼센트 성립하려면 영단어 하나마다 반드시 그에 대응하는 우리말 단어(혹은 단어군)가 존재해야만 합니다. 다시 말해 영어와 우리말 사이에 완전한 대응관계가 성립되어야 하지요.

그러나 안타깝게도 우리나라와 영어권 나라들은 풍토, 문화, 종교, 역사가 전혀 다른 나라들입니다. 그런 대응 관계가 성립될 리 없지요. 그럼에도 억지로 영어를 우리말로 일일이 번역하려 들면 어쩔 수 없이 의미의 왜곡이 발생합니다. 의미가 왜곡되면서 벌어진 틈 사이로 중요한 요소가 새어나가버리기도 하죠.

이번 해설에서는 번역시 발생하는 의미의 왜곡, 그 '잃어버린 영역'으로 한 걸음 다가가 외국어를 배우는 참된 의미, 그리고 일상생활의 상식조차 바뀌어버리는 외국어의 오묘한 재미를 철저히 해부하려고 합니다.

자, 그럼 드디어 '잃어버린 영역'으로 출발해볼까요?

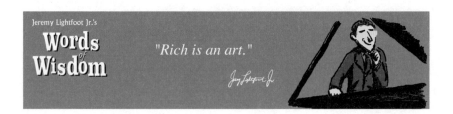

Jeremy Lightfoot Jr.'s
Words of Wisdom

"Rich is an art."

'study'를 공부하다

'공부하다'는 아마 좀 부담이 느껴지는 단어일 것입니다. 이 단어를 영어로 번역한다면 어떤 단어가 가장 먼저 떠오를까요? 제일 먼저 study가 생각날 거예요. 그러나 study에 실제로 '공부한다'는 의미가 있을까요?

우리나라 사람이 '공부한다'고 할 때 느끼는 다소 부담스럽고 하기 싫은 이미지가 영어의 study에는 없습니다. study는 왠지 '공부하다'보다 더 '거창한 느낌'이 드는 단어예요.

예를 들어 study를 문장 중에서 써보세요.

1. I studied English in high school.

2. I studied the crime scene.

1번 문장을 우리말로 번역하면 '나는 고등학교 때 영어를 공부했다'라는 문장이 돼요. 분명 우리말의 '공부하다'와 의미가 똑같습니다. 그러나 2번 문장을 번역하면 '나는 범행 현장을 조사했다'란 문장이 되므로 이미지가 상당히 달라져요.

우리나라의 '공부하다'라는 단어에는 암기나 계산을 꾸준히 해나가는 이미지가 있는 반면 영어의 study란 단어에는 '연구하다'나 '관찰하다'와 같이 더 깊은 의미가 담겨 있기 때문이에요. 이렇게 이미지에 차이가 있으므로, 초등학생이 하는 공부처럼 study라고 하기엔 너무 단순한 경우에는 일반적으로 work를 쓴답니다.

한편 이 work를 우리말로 직역하면 '일하다'란 의미가 됩니다. 수학 문제를 풀고 있는 아이가 '일하고 있다'라고 표현하기엔 사실 어딘가 어색하게 느껴지지요. 그 이유는 우리말의 '일하다'란 단어는 '보수를 받고 노동을 한다'는 이미지가 강한 반면에 영어의 work는 '단순한 작업을 반복한다'는 이미지가 있기 때문이에요. 둘 사이에는 이런 미묘한 차이가 있습니다.

| 공부하다 | study | 일하다 | work |

'공부하다'와 study, '일하다'와 work. 사전에는 분명히 의미가 같다고 나와 있지요. 하지만 사실상 쓰임에는 상당한 차이가 있습니다. study와 '공부하다'의 공통된 이미지는 '무슨 일인가를 배우다'의 정도로 실제로 하는 작업에는 큰 차이가 있답니다.

설명이 까다로우므로 이들 단어의 차이를 알기 쉽게 그림으로 나타내볼게요.

예를 들어 우리말의 '공부하다'가 포함하고 있는 모든 요소를 파란 원으로 나타내보세요.

BFC JUMBLE

Unscramble the words, then collect the letters in the circle.
Unscramble once more to find the answer to the quiz!

Q: Ed has forgotten something. What?

A: The cat's ◯◯◯◯◯◯

이번에는 영어의 study가 포함하고 있는 모든 요소를 노란 원으로 나타내볼게요.

이 두 단어의 의미가 완전히 일치한다면 파란 원과 노란 원이 정확히 하나로 겹쳐지겠지만 실제로는 다음과 같이 겹쳐지게 됩니다.

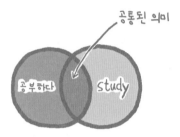

겹치는 부분의 테두리 안에만 공통된 의미가 있고, 나머지 부분은 의미가 전혀 다른 별개의 단어인 셈입니다. 사전에 일단 의미가 같은 단어라고 나와 있어도 실제로는 겹치는 부분이 많은 단어가 있는가 하면 전혀 겹치는 부분이 없는 단어도 있어요. 또한 원이 정확히 하나로 겹쳐지는 단어는 단 한 개도 없습니다. '사과'와 apple처럼 의미가 단 하나뿐이라고 생각하는 단어조차 원이 약간은 어긋나게 겹쳐져요.

BFC JUMBLE

#1 RYHUR

#2 EUVANE

#3 DUTARMS

#4 PALCOLES

사과   apple

　결국 번역이란 겹치는 부분의 의미만을 취하고, 나머지 부분은 버리는 것입니다. 이 버려진 부분에 담긴 의미나 뉘앙스, 글쓴이의 감정은 번역하는 순간 '잃어버린 영역'으로 사라져버리는 셈이지요. 그러므로 겉으로 드러난 표면상의 의미만으로 원문의 생각을 파악하려고 해서는 영문을 제대로 이해할 수 없습니다.

　만약 번역만으로 모든 문제가 해결된다면, result나 consequence처럼 우리말로 옮겼을 때 같은 의미가 되어버리는 단어(두 단어 모두 우리말로는 '결과')를 영어권 나라 사람들이 굳이 구분해서 쓰는 이유를 영원히 알 수 없게 되겠지요. 우리말로는 같은 단어로 번역되는데도 그들에게는 그 둘의 뜻이 전혀 다른 단어인 것이니까요.

웃음의 종류

　그럼, 극단적인 예를 하나 소개하겠습니다. 바로 '웃다'란 단어예요. 우리말로 '웃다'라고 하면

이런 동작도……

이런 동작도……

이런 동작도……

모두 우리말의 '웃다'에 해당하지요.

그러나 위에서 나열한 동작을 영어로 옮기면 놀랄 만큼 상황이 달라진답니다. 왜냐하면 영어는 '웃다'란 하나의 동작을 다음과 같이 다양한 단어로 구분해서 쓰기 때문이에요.

laugh
소리를 내서 웃다

smile
미소를 띠다

sneer
냉소적으로 웃다

smirk
음흉한 속셈이 담긴 웃음

giggle
깔깔 웃다

chuckle
억누르는 웃음

crack up
함박웃음

ridicule
웃음거리로 만들다

jeer
빈정거리며 야유하다

mock
(상대의 흉내 등을 내며) 놀리다

Ingredients

(for the crust)
150g graham crackers
3 tablespoons soft brown sugar
1/3 cup melted butter or margarine

(for the filling)
2/3 cup sugar
1/3 cup melted butter or margarine
1 cup corn syrup
3 eggs
1/2 teaspoon salt
1 cup pecan nuts

깜짝 놀라지는 않았나요? 하지만 아직 끝이 아니랍니다. 사실은 좀 더 많이 있어요. 이 중에서 회화에 자주 쓰이는 단어는 smile, laugh, giggle, crack up 정도지만 문장을 읽다 보면 다른 단어도 종종 볼 수 있습니다.

우리말의 '웃다'는 이 중에서 laugh로 생각하기 쉽지만, 우리말의 '웃다'가 훨씬 폭넓게 쓰이는 말이에요. 영어의 laugh는 '하하하하!' 하고 경쾌하고 즐겁게 소리를 내면서 웃을 때만 사용하는 단어지만, 우리말에서는 얼굴에 웃음기가 나타나면 대부분 '웃다'라고 표현할 수 있어요.

그림으로 나타내면 다음과 같습니다.

또 ridicule, jeer, mock, 이 세 단어를 자세히 살펴보면 우리말과 영어의 '웃음'에 어떤 차이가 있는지 좀 더 분명하게 드러납니다. 이 단어들이 나타내는 '웃는 방식'의 차이를 우리말로 표현했을 때 사실 '비웃다, 조롱하다' 이외의 말로는 표현하기 힘들어요. 하지만 ridicule은 '상대를 웃음거리로 만드는 상황'을 가리키고, jeer는 '야, 야 하면서 따돌림 당하는 아이를 비웃는 상황'을 말하며 mock는 '상대를 바보 취급하며 코웃음 치는 상황'을 나타냅니다. 이처럼 실로 미묘한 차이가 있어서 세 단어는 각각 별개의 상태를 나타내요.

이런 미묘한 차이는 우리나라 사람이 이해하기가 매우 어렵습니다. 원래 우리나라 사람들은 위의 세 가지 상황을 구별하지 않으므로, 명확히 어떤 상황에서 어느 단어를 선택해야 하는지 알 수 없기 때문이지요. 또한 어쨌든 이런 모든 단어가 우리말로는 기본적으로 '웃다'라는 한 단어로 집약되기 때문입니다. 그림으로 나타내면 다음과 같은 느낌 아닐까요.

1. Crush the graham crackers into crumbs. Mix the soft brown sugar and melted butter into the crackers and mix well. Spread in pie dish. Press mixture with fingers until thin to form the piecrust. Cool in refrigerator.

참고로 이 그림에서 각각의 원들이 '웃다'란 원에서 조금씩 비어져 나온 이유는 laugh도 jeer도 mock도 ridicule도 '웃다'란 단어에는 없는 의미나 뉘앙스를 조금씩 담고 있기 때문입니다. 역시 어떤 경우라도 원이 정확히 하나로 겹쳐질 수는 없어요.

더 쉬운 예를 몇 개 들어볼게요.
우리말로는 화살표가 가리키는 부분을 무엇이라고 할까요?

2. Heat oven to 190℃. Beat sugar, melted butter, corn syrup, salt and eggs in medium bowl with hand beater until well blended. Stir in pecans.

그렇다면 이 그림은요?

우리말로는 턱에 난 '수염'도 수염이고 코 밑에 난 '수염'도 수염입니다. 수염 앞에 턱이나 코를 붙여서 턱수염, 콧수염으로 구분하기는 하지만 영어가 모국어인 사람은 턱수염을 beard, 콧수염을 mustache라고 별개의 단어로 쓰지요. beard와 mustache를 동시에 표현하는 영단어는 없어요. beard와 mustache가 영어에서는 서로 다른 별개의 신체 영역으로 취급되기 때문입니다.

지금까지는 무심코 지나쳐왔지만 언뜻 단순한 단어로 보여도 속뜻을 살펴보면 이처럼 '우리말과 다른 차이'가 잔뜩 숨겨져 있습니다.

예를 들어 '어리광을 부리다'란 단어가 영어에는 없어요. 왜냐하면 '어리광을 부리다'란 사고 자체가 영미권 사람들에게는 존재하지 않기 때문이지요. 아이가 부모한테 어리광을 부리는 경우에 해당하는 표현은 있지만, 자립심이 강한 영미권에서는 어른이 어른에게 어리광을 부리는 행위 자체가 이해 불가능한 행위입니다. 당연히 이런 행위를 표현하는 단어 자체도 존재하지 않아요. 따라서 우리나라 사람이 봤을 때는 '어리광을 부리는 행위'가 그들의 눈에는

3. Pour into pie plate. Bake 40 ~ 50 minutes or until lightly brown. Cover with foil if crust starts to burn. Serve warm.

그저 '기대고 있다'거나 부정적인 시각으로 보면 '얼렁뚱땅 넘어가려고 한다'와 같이 의미가 전혀 다른 행위로 보이지요.

우리가 볼 때는 '(여학생이 남학생에게) 어리광을 부리고 있다'   영미권 사람들이 볼 때는 '(남녀가 서로) 기대고 있다'

　　또 다른 예를 들어볼게요. 우리나라의 색연필 세트에는 대개 '살색'이라고 불리는, 연한 베이지 비슷한 색이 포함되어 있었지요. 하지만 다민족 국가에서는 '살색'이란 개념이 모호하기 때문에 살색 색연필은 존재하지 않습니다.

　　우리나라에서도 '살색'을 살구색으로 바꾸어 부르고 있지요. 영어로는 이 색을 뭐라고 할까요? 답은 peach예요. peach는 과일인 '복숭아'를 일컫지만, 복숭아 안쪽의 연한 베이지 계통의 색은 '살구색'과 확실히 비슷해요.

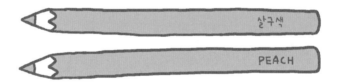

　　이제 살구색이 peach에 해당한다는 사실은 알았지만, 생각해보아야 할 문제가 여전히 남아 있습니다. 우리말에도 '복숭앗빛'이란 표현이 있기 때문이에요. 우리말의 복숭앗빛은 베이지보다는 분홍에 가까워요. 그리고 '분홍'은 영어의 pink로 또 다른 색입니다.

이런 점을 생각해보면 평소 당연하다고 여겼던 상식의 틀이 얼마나 깨지기 쉬운 것인지 깨닫게 됩니다. 동작의 구분도 사물의 이름도 색의 차이도 사실은 확고부동한 진리가 아닙니다. 외국어를 배우는 묘미는 어쩌면 바로 이런 사실을 깨치는 데 있을지도 몰라요.

어쩔 수 없이 인간은 세상에 존재하는 사물과 동작과 개념을 모국어의 틀 안에서 받아들이기 쉽습니다. 대상을 모국어의 관점으로만 파악하는 것이니까요. 그러나 언어가 바뀌면 대상을 규정짓는 틀이 의외로 쉽게 무너져버리고 지금껏 알고 있던 상식이 통하지 않게 돼요.

외국어를 배우다 보면 이런 당황스런 경험을 여러 번 겪게 된답니다. 어찌된 셈인지 외국어를 배우면서도 단어의 발음만 다를 뿐 대상을 규정짓는 틀은 같으리라고 착각하기 쉽습니다. 그러나 외국어를 배운다는 것은 단순히 단어장에 나온 단어들을 잔뜩 암기하는 것이 아니라 세상의 모든 사물을 바라보는 관점을 새롭게 바꾸는 것이지요. 지금까지 이름이 없던 사물에 이름이 생길 수도 있고, 반대로 이름이 사라지는 경우도 있습니다.

외국어를 배운다는 것은 백지상태였던 어린 시절로 되돌아가서 세상에 존재하는 사물의 이름을 다시 새롭게 익히는 과정입니다. 미지의 세계인 '잃어버린 영역'을 찾아 떠나는 모험이 시작되는 것이에요.

이름이 없는 사물

사물의 이름을 새롭게 익히는 과정에서, '이제까지 이름이 없던 사물에 이름을 붙이는 일'은 매우 신기한 경험일 것입니다. 희귀한 수입품이나 우리나라에는 존재하지 않는 제품을 일컫는 경우를 말하는 것이 아닙니다. 아주 흔하고 일상적인 동작이나 감각 중에서도 우리말로는 딱히 정해진 표현이 없을 때가 의외로 많아요.

reputation이란 단어를 예로 들어볼게요.

reputation은 '지금까지 계속 어떤 일을 특정한 방식으로 해왔으므로 당연히 이번에도 이전과 같은 방식으로 하리라는 생각'으로 우리말로 의미를 따지면 다소 복잡해집니다. 우리말로는 reputation에 딱 들어맞는 일상적인 단어가 없으니까요. 잠시 제레미를 통해서 실제로 이 단어를 사용해볼게요.

이건 하지 않는 게 좋다고 생각해 .　　걱정 마. 난 이런 일을 할 거라는　　으아아아아아악!
　　　　　　　　　　　　　　　　　reputation이 있거든.

이 문장의 reputation을 우리말로 바꿔볼게요. 굳이 끼워 맞추면 '평판'이나 '명성' 정도가 되겠지만, 이 단어들은 둘 다 비교적 긍정적인 이미지가 있으므로 영어의 reputation과는 받아들이는 인상이 상당히 많이 달라집니다. reputation에는 가장 중요한 뉘앙스로 '평가가 원래 나빴으니까 더 이상 나빠질 것도 없다'와 같은 의미가 있기 때문이에요. 즉 이미 악평이 난 마당에 평가를 두려워할 까닭이 없다는 속뜻이 '잃어버린 영역'에 숨어 있는 셈이지요.

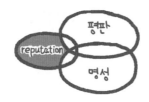

이외에도 '뉘앙스', '이미지', '모티베이션' 등 우리말로는 딱 떨어지는 표현이 없어서 외래어로 자주 쓰이는 단어들이 많이 있습니다. '모티베이션'을 번역하면 '동기 부여'가 되지만 동기 부여란 단어만 봐서는 '긍정적인 에너지가 바탕이 된 동기'라는 활기찬 느낌이 전달되지 않아요. 이런 단어들은 영단어의 의미를 잘 알고 있는 사람이 우리말을 할 때도 그 느낌을 고스란히 전달하기 위해 무리해서 사용하다 보니 결국 외래어로 정착한 것이에요.

한편 우리말을 영어로 옮길 때 사라져버리는 부분도 있습니다. 예를 들어 영어는 '무언가에 부딪힐 때 나는 소리'를 나타내는 단어가 slam이나 crash 정도지만, 우리말에는 무수히 많아요. 쾅, 꽈당, 탁, 퍽, 팍 등 다채로운 소리나 의성어들은 영어로 옮기는 순간 전부 사라져버려요.

우리말로는 전혀 다르게 표현되는 소리도 영어로는 모두 똑같은 하나의 소리가 되고 만다.

한편 영어에는 강조하는 단어가 많이 있습니다. 우리말로는 '정말 대단해'나 '끝내줘' 정도
가 최상급 표현이지만 영어로는 슬랭까지 포함해서 세분화하다 보면 10단계 정도로 매우 과
장된 표현까지 준비되어 있지요. 따라서 '끝내줘'보다 강도가 강한 표현이 영어로 나오면 우리
말로 아무리 강조하려고 해도 번역하는 순간 전부 '끝내줘' 정도의 수준으로 떨어지고 맙니
다. 그 이상 격렬한 감정을 표현하는 단어가 우리말에는 없기 때문이에요. 이 경우도 번역하면
서 '잃어버린 영역'으로 표류하게 되는 부분입니다.

넌 대단해!
You're great!

넌 정말 대단해!
You're really
great!

넌 끝내줘!
You're
incredible!

(동급 표현 없음)
You're amazing!

(동급 표현 없음)
You're
unbelievable!

(동급 표현 없음)
You're goddamn
great!

(동급 표현 없음)
You're!
(방송 금지이므로 게재 불가!)

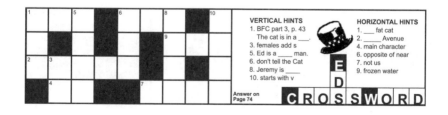

VERTICAL HINTS
1. BFC part 3, p. 43 The cat is in a ___.
3. females add s
5. Ed is a ___ man.
6. don't tell the Cat
8. Jeremy is ___
10. starts with v

HORIZONTAL HINTS
1. ___ fat cat
2. ___ Avenue
4. main character
6. opposite of near
7. not us
9. frozen water

Answer on Page 74

CROSSWORD

　이런 '잃어버린 영역'에 자리하고 있는 요소들은 매우 중요한 의미를 가지고 있는데도 불구하고 사전에 실릴 수도, 학교에서 가르쳐줄 수도 없습니다. 왜냐하면 이 부분은 시대와 장소에 따라 자꾸 바뀌는 애매한 속성, 다시 말해 각 단어의 '이미지'에 해당하기 때문이에요.

　평소에는 그다지 의식하지 못하지만 모든 단어는 '의미' 이외에 '이미지'를 지니고 있습니다. 사전에는 '의미'만 실려 있지만 단어의 '이미지'는 매우 중요한 부분이에요. '이 단어는 어떤 타입의 사람이 언제 어떤 감정으로 누구에게 사용하고 어떤 효과를 불러일으킬까······.' 이런 요소는 번역하는 과정에서 결국에는 사라져버려요. 단어 차원에서도 이러하니 문장 차원이 되면 더욱 많은 요소를 잃어버리게 되지요.

　예를 들어 다음 문장을 살펴볼게요.

She is expecting a baby.

　expect의 의미는 대부분 사전에 '기대하다'로 씌어져 있습니다. 이 문장을 그대로 번역하면 '그녀는 아기를 기대하고 있다'가 돼요.

　의미상으로는 번역문도 영어와 일치합니다. 단 잃어버린 요소가 있습니다. 번역하고 나니 기대의 '강도'가 어느 정도인지 알 수 없게 되어버린 것이지요.

우리말만 봐서는 막연히 아기를 원하고 있다는 정도에 불과합니다. 그러나 영어 문장은 막연히 아이를 원하는 정도가 아니라 아이가 세상에 나올 날을 확신하면서 기다리고 있다는 말입니다. 즉 이 문장은 이미 임신을 한 상태라는 사실과 머지않아 출산하리라는 사실, 두 가지 사실을 동시에 알려주는 말이에요.

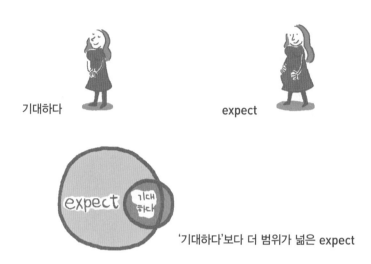

기대하다   expect

'기대하다'보다 더 범위가 넓은 expect

'이미지'가 불러일으키는 영향력은 때에 따라서는 '의미' 이상으로 큽니다. 하나의 단어를 제대로 암기한다는 것은, 단순히 그 단어의 표면적인 의미만을 암기하는 것이 아니라 그 단어의 이미지가 머리에 확실히 인식될 때까지 다양한 상황에서 같은 단어를 수차례 접하면서 인상을 파악해가는 것이에요. 단어를 머리가 아닌 마음으로 받아들이는 것이지요. Big Fat Cat 시리즈를 통해서 영어책, 특히 영어 소설을 읽으라고 반복해서 말한 결정적인 이유가 바로 여기에 있답니다.

"TRUST OUR CRUST!"
STATE PIE FESTIVAL
HELD AT THE NEW EVERVILLE MALL DEC.15-24 A.M.9:00-P.M.7:00

'의미'만 알고 '이미지'를 모르는 단어는 결코 제대로 사용할 수 없습니다. 마음에 '이미지'가 남아 있는 단어만이 자신에게 살아 있는 단어랍니다.

laugh란 단어를 암기할 때 단순히 'laugh=웃다'라고 해서는 laugh에 담긴 '가벼움, 경쾌한 웃음'이란 이미지가 '잃어버린 영역'으로 사라지고 말지요. 의미만 암기한 laugh는 영미권 사람들이 구사하는 laugh에 비해 많은 요소가 희석되어버려요. laugh란 단어를 암기할 때는 누군가 웃는 모습을 머리에 그려야 해요. 이렇게 이미지를 그리는 노력이 꼭 필요합니다. '웃다'라는 우리말이 머리에 떠오른다고 해도 '웃다'는 결코 laugh가 아닙니다. 'laugh하고 있는 이미지'가 떠오를 때 비로소 영어를 모국어로 구사하고 있는 사람들의 감각이 몸에 배는 것이지요.

The cat scratched Ed.

지금까지 여러분은 Big Fat Cat 시리즈를 꾸준히 읽어왔기 때문에 이 문장을 보면 머리에 어떤 그림이 떠오를 거예요. 이렇게 자연스럽게 머리에 떠오른다면 단어들을 제대로 암기했다고 볼 수 있습니다. 바로 이 느낌이 단어를 머리가 아니라 마음으로 받아들이는 것이에요. 이런 느낌은 '의미'가 아닙니다! '이미지'이지요!

외워야겠다고 의식하면서 읽을 필요 없습니다. 즐기면서 읽기만 해도 충분해요. 단어의 이미지는 많은 책을 읽다 보면 저절로 마음에 남습니다. 입으로 들어간 음식물이 의식하지 않아도 체내로 흡수되어 영양분으로 바뀌듯이 지식도 필요한 분량만큼 신체가 선별해서 흡수해요.

영어와 우리말은 비슷해 보여도 많은 차이가 있습니다. 그러므로 '영어 학습=영어를 우리말로 바꾼다'라는 생각은 너무나 안일한 사고방식이에요. 번역할 때는 'cry=울다'와 같은 단어 바꾸기만이 아니라, 다음 그림같이 스스로 결코 잊을 수 없는 이미지로 바꿔보길 바랍니다.

바로 이런 과정을 위해서 에드와 고양이와 제레미와 윌리가 존재해요. 세상의 모든 이야기 속 캐릭터들은 잃어버린 영역을 찾아서 책의 세계로 독자가 들어오기만을 기다리고 있습니다.

외국어를 배운다는 것의 참의미

그러나 '이미지'가 자리 잡을 때까지는 그 단어를 이해하기 위한 방편으로써 우리말로 번역해보는 것도 한 방법입니다. 그러나 이 단계에 그쳐서는 안 돼요. 우리말 번역으로 그치면 어쩔 수 없이 '잃어버린 영역'이 생겨버려요.

이 '잃어버린 영역'을 스스로 메울 수 있는 편리한 도구가 사전입니다. 하지만 사전은 사용법이 잘못 알려진 경우가 많은 도구이기도 하지요.

사전에는 대개 한 단어에 대해서 다양한 뜻풀이가 실려 있습니다. 사전을 펼쳤을 때 만약 세 개의 뜻풀이가 실려 있다면 대부분의 사람들은 그 세 개 중에서 가장 적합한 뜻풀이를 선택하려고 합니다. 그러나 사전에 다양한 뜻풀이를 실은 이유는 '이 중에서 고르라'는 말이 아닙니다. 다양한 뜻풀이를 종합적으로 고려해야 그 단어의 의미를 제대로 파악할 수 있다는 말이지요.

예를 들어 run이란 단어를 사전에서 찾아볼게요. 몇 가지 의미가 있을 거예요. 그러면 우리

Jeremy Lightfoot Jr.'s
Words of **Wisdom**

"The three important things in life:
Love, money, and the love of money."

는 보통 'run에는 이렇게 여러 가지 뜻이 있군' 정도로만 생각해요. 하지만 아래와 같은 형태로 생각해보세요.

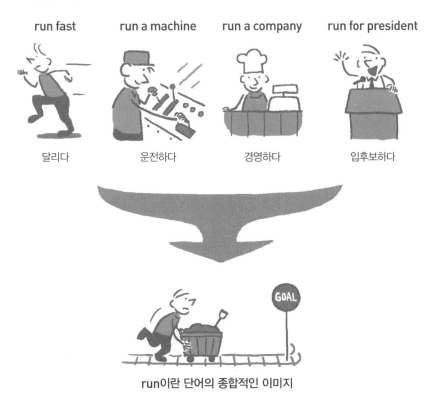

run이란 단어의 종합적인 이미지

다른 문화권에서는 한 단어로 표현할 수 있는 대상이지만, 우리말로는 여러 단어를 동원해야만 제대로 표현할 수 있기 때문에 사전에 다양한 뜻풀이를 나열해놓은 거예요. 사전을 펼쳐

볼 때는 다양한 뜻풀이를 보면서 왼쪽 그림과 같은 요령으로 '대략 종합하면 이런 이미지'라고 감을 잡고 다시 영어의 세계로 돌아가도록 합니다. 이 방법이 사전의 참된 활용법이에요.

하지만 될 수 있는 한 사전을 펼치기 전에 전후 관계나 스토리, 등장인물의 성격이나 이야기의 전개 등을 살펴보고 모르는 단어의 의미를 상상해보세요. 이렇게 하면 이미지가 훨씬 더 잘 그려질 거예요. 그런 다음 사전을 찾아보면 매우 효과적입니다.

영어책을 읽을 때 사전을 찾는 방법에도 약간의 요령이 있습니다. 부디 참고하기 바랍니다.

(1) 처음 읽을 때는 다소 무리가 되더라도 사전을 펼치지 말고(아무리 해도 사전이 필요하다면 최소한으로 한정지을 것) 두 번째 읽을 때 모르는 단어에 밑줄을 긋는다.
(2) 모르는 단어는 여러 페이지에 걸쳐서 미리 뜻을 달아두고 사전은 덮어두고 읽는다.
(3) 번역문이 있으면 미리 번역문을 읽고 스토리를 이해한 다음 다시 한번 영어로 읽는다.

어느 방법이나 상관없지만, 될 수 있는 한 (1)의 방법을 권장하고 싶습니다. 만약 (1)의 방법으로는 모르는 단어가 너무 많아서 도저히 읽기 힘들다면 주저 없이 그 책은 다음 기회로 미루고 난이도가 더 쉬운 책에 도전해보세요. 처음에는 쉬운 책부터 읽는 것도 좋은 방법입니다.

무리해서 영화의 원작소설을 읽기보다는 가벼운 마음으로 그림책을 읽어보길 바랍니다. '이 나이에 무슨 그림책?!'이라고 생각할지 모르겠지만, 그림책은 어린이들만 보는 책이 결코 아니에요. 영어 그림책 중에는 어른이 읽어도 흥미진진한 책이 많이 있습니다. 시험 삼아 몇 권 읽어보고 그림책이 어린이만 읽는 책인지 아닌지 스스로 판단해보세요.

영어학습법은 무수히 많습니다. 절대적으로 옳거나 틀린 방법은 없어요. 자신에게 맞는다고 느끼면 망설이지 말고 시험해보길 바랍니다. 어떤 학습법이든 즐길 수 있다면 그 방법이 최고예요. 영어를 즐길 수 있다면 그것으로 충분하답니다.

번역을 하면서 잃어버리는 것들. 그것들을 찾아서 여기까지 왔습니다. 잃어버린 요소는 때에 따라서 화자의 '개성'이나 '감정'일 수도 있고 '가치관'이 될 수도 있습니다. 또는 '국민성', '습관', '사고방식'일 수도 있어요. '재치 있는 표현'이나 '다정한 말투'가 사라지는 경우도 있지요.

하지만 훨씬 더 간단하고 쉬운 단어로 이런 '잃어버린 요소' 전체를 표현할 수 있습니다.

잃어버린 것은 바로 화자의 '마음'입니다.

단어에 이미지가 있는 한, 그 단어를 선택한 화자의 마음이 단어에 묻어나는 것은 당연한 이치입니다. 그 사람은 그 단어가 아니면 안 되기 때문에 그 단어를 선택한 것이지요. 아무리 비슷한 단어나 대체할 만한 표현이 있다고 해도 자신의 기분을 그 단어를 썼을 때만큼 제대로 표현할 수는 없어요.

영어는 살아 있습니다. 지금 이 순간에도 세계 어느 곳에선 누군가 영어를 쓰고 있어요. 그리고 그 사람들은 사전에 나온 대로 말하거나 문법에 얽매여 영어를 쓰지는 않는답니다. 문장을 쓰는 도중에 기분에 따라 갑자기 표현을 바꾸기도 하고 단어의 의미를 착각하기도 하고 새로운 단어를 지어내기도 하지요. 따라서 영어를 이해하려고 할 때 사전이나 문법에 기대면 당연히 한계에 부딪힐 수밖에 없습니다.

'영어' 자체를 이해하는 것은 사실 간단합니다. 그러나 사람을 이해하는 것은 한국인이든 미국인이든 어느 나라 사람이든 어려운 일이에요. 게다가 익숙지 않은 언어로 대화해야 한다면 더욱 어려워져요.

외국어가 어려운 이유는 대부분 언어 능력이나 이해력 부족 때문이 아니라 사람과 사람 사이의 커뮤니케이션이 원래 어렵기 때문입니다. 사람마다 자라온 환경과 문화적 배경이 다르므로 어찌 보면 당연한 결과입니다. 커뮤니케이션이 어려운 이유를 외국어 때문이라고 생각하기 쉽지만 우리나라 사람끼리 대화를 한다고 해도 상대의 진심을 얼마나 파악할 수 있을까요? 이때는 언어 장벽 때문이라고 '언어'를 핑계 삼을 수도 없습니다. 그러니 '연령'이나 '성

별', 또는 '개성'이나 '지위' 등을 핑계 삼지요.

커뮤니케이션에서 중요한 것은 언어 그 자체가 아닙니다. 영어를 배울 때도 마찬가지예요. 영어가 커뮤니케이션을 가로막는 장벽이 되어서는 안 돼요. 오히려 영어는 문화와 세계관이 다른 사람을 이해하기 위한 소중한 매개체입니다. 즉 다른 문화권에 속한 사람을 이해하기 위해 영어를 배우는 것이지요.

영어든 어느 나라 말이든 언어는 변하지 않는 것이 아니라 살아서 움직입니다. 따라서 애매모호하고 좀처럼 손에 잘 잡히지 않는 것이에요. 하지만 바로 이런 속성 때문에 어느 시대, 어느 곳에 있든지 사람의 마음을 전달할 수 있는 도구가 돼요. 이런 변화무쌍하고 애매모호한 언어를 확고부동한 것으로 바꾸려 하거나 심지어 점수로 환산하는 것은 불가능합니다. 따라서 조금 이해하기 어려운 부분이 있어도 영어를 영어 그 자체로 받아들이는 여유가 필요하지요. 영어가 살아서 움직일 수 있는 여지를 남겨두길 바랍니다. 그렇게 할 때 영어가 마음속에서 성장하고 진화하며 토대를 넓혀갈 수 있어요.

영어를 그 자체로 받아들이는 여유가 있을 때 비로소 영어다운 영어를 구사할 수 있습니다. 이런 여유가 '잃어버린 영역'으로 사라져버리려는 화자의 마음을 되살리고요. '화자의 마음'을 잃어버린 영역으로 놓쳐버릴지 되살릴지는 언제나 자신에게 달려 있답니다.

TIPS FROM THE CAT:
영어식 표현 뒤에 숨어 있는 속뜻을 찾아서

영어 소설을 술술 읽기 위해
Big Fat Cat이 살짝 알려주는 도움말입니다.
이번에는 본문의 '관용구'에 숨어 있는
속뜻을 명쾌하게 밝혔으니 어서 들어오세요.

〈Big Fat Cat vs. Mr. Jones〉를 재밌게 읽으셨나요? 이제 Big Fat Cat 시리즈도 5권에 접어들어 에드와 고양이의 모험이 절정을 향해 치닫고 있습니다.

그런데 눈치 채셨어요? 이번 본문에는 몇 군데 ※ 표시가 붙은 곳이 있습니다. 이 표시가 붙은 부분은 4권 해설에 등장했던 '관용구'의 일종입니다. 의미를 알고 있으면 아주 재미있는 표현이 되지만 의미를 모르면 아무리 생각해도 속뜻을 알 수 없는 문장들이지요.

지금까지 Big Fat Cat 시리즈에서는 읽기 쉬운 문장이 되도록 가능한 이런 표현을 자제해 왔지만 관용구도 영어의 묘미를 느낄 수 있는 한 부분이므로 이번 작품부터는 조금씩 첨가했습니다.

하지만 이야기 전개상 중요한 부분은 아니므로 처음에 읽을 때는 건너뛰고 두 번째 읽을 때부터 의미를 살펴봐도 괜찮습니다. 만약 여유가 있다면 퀴즈를 푸는 듯한 기분으로 관용구의 의미를 먼저 상상해본 뒤에 이 페이지를 읽으면 색다른 재미를 느낄 수 있을 겁니다.

그럼 이번 작품에 등장한 관용구의 속뜻을 알아봅시다.

the time draws near (p.17)

draw는 상당히 폭넓은 의미가 있는 화살표로, 우리말에는 없는 단어입니다. 우리말로 번역하면 '(그림을) 그리다'란 단어가 가장 먼저 떠오르지만, 원래는 '잡아당기다'란 의미예요. '선을 잡아당겨 긋다'가 진화하여 '그리다'가 된 거예요. 이 문장에서 잡아당기는 주체는 time입니다. 미래의 마감 시간이 조금씩 현재로 다가오고 있다는 말로, 살짝 긴장감을 주면서 임박한 시간을 나타냈어요. 참고로 pull에도 '잡아당기다'란 의미가 있지만 draw와는 차이가 있지요. draw는 제비뽑기처럼 '뽑아서 선택하다'라는 뉘앙스가 있습니다.

a trick of the eye (p.18)

말 그대로 '눈속임'입니다. 자신의 눈이 자신에게 장난(트릭)을 걸고 있네요. 다시 말해 '눈의 착각'이란 의미입니다.

going crazy (p.24)

crazy는 일반적으로 '미친 상태'를 가리킵니다. '광기'로 go하고 있다면 그다지 좋은 의미로 들리지는 않지만 crazy에는 다소 유머러스하게 '미쳐 있어도 활력은 넘친다'라는 긍정적인 요소가 담겨 있습니다. 이 문장에서는 미쳤다고 할 만큼 시끌벅적하고 성황을 이루는 모습을 아나운서가 이렇게 표현했어요.

sort of rings a bell (p.29)

무언가를 '생각해낸다'거나 '떠올린다'고 할 때 만화에서는 주로 머리 위에 전구가 켜지는 모습으로 표현합니다. 영어 문장에서는 '종을 울리다'란 관용구가 이런 표현에 해당해요. sort of는 우리말의 '왠지 모르게'에 해당하는 단어예요.

Holy cow / Holy macaroni (p.29/p.31)

깊은 의미는 없습니다. 미국에서는 Holy(성스럽다)에 엉뚱한 단어를 붙여서 놀람을 나타내는 경우가 흔해요. 마카로니나 소(cow)는 운율도 맞아 떨어져서 자주 쓰여요. 이외에도 Holy cat 등 여러 가지 패턴이 있습니다.

all for the best (p.39)

이 문장과 가장 가까운 우리말은 '끝이 좋으면 다 좋다'입니다. '좋은 일도 나쁜 일도 모두 다 포함해서 마지막은 좋은 방향으로 갔다'란 의미로 자주 쓰이는 관용구예요. 약간 강도를 약화해서 all for the better라고도 합니다.

관용구는 속담과 같아서 일상 회화에 악센트를 살짝 더합니다. 의미를 알고 있으면 매우 편리하지만 너무 많이 인용하면 속담이나 고사성어를 연발할 때처럼 어색한 인상을 주지요. 그러므로 일부러 관용구 목록을 만들어서 암기할 필요는 없습니다. 다만 글이나 대화 중에 나올 때마다 자연스럽게 익히는 편이 낫습니다. 이렇게 하면 어떤 관용구가 어떤 사람에게 어느 정도 빈도로 사용되는지도 알게 된답니다.

BFC SPECIAL FEATURE:

A NIGHT AT THE CINEMA

Script by Takahiko Mukoyama
Breakdowns by Yoji Takemura
Art by Tetsuo Takashima

POPCORN?

THE SMELL.

THE SWEET SMELL.

IT ALSO TASTES SWEET.

LOOK, KID. I KNOW YOU HAVE TO LIVE. BUT GO EASY ON THE GUN, OKAY?

SOMETIMES IT DOES HIT.

HERE'S A SOUVENIR FOR YOU.

THE WORLD IS A COLD PLACE.

WELL... MOST OF IT ANYWAY.

알파벳으로 씌어진 글은 뭐든지 한마디로 영어라고 하지만 영어에도 여러 종류가 있습니다. Big Fat Cat 시리즈의 본문은 정통 내레이션 기법을 쓰고 있지만 다른 문체를 접해보는 것도 색다른 경험이 될 듯합니다. 이번에 수록한 〈A Night at the Cinema〉는 만화 형식에 절제된 독백조 내레이션을 곁들였지요. 하드보일드 소설에서 자주 보이는 문체로 다소 난이도가 높은 문형입니다. 이런 문체는 분위기를 중시하므로 단어의 뜻풀이도 일부러 달지 않았습니다. 아마 당황한 분들도 많이 있을 거예요. 이해하기 어려운 경우, 본문에 나오는 문장이 크게 세 종류임을 알아두면 한결 쉬워질 겁니다.

1. 목소리를 내서 말하는 일반 대화문. (말풍선 안에 있는 문장)
2. 주인공이 내레이터가 되어서 자신의 인생을 객관적으로 서술하는 문장.
   (자신을 You라고 부르며 서술한 문장. 84쪽 첫 번째 칸 문장 등)
3. 현장에서 떠오른 주인공의 생각을 그대로 서술한 짧은 문장.
   (84쪽 세 번째 칸 문장 등)

또 전체를 관통하는 두 개의 핵심 키워드에 주목하면 이야기의 흐름을 쉽게 파악할 수 있을 거예요.

pain: 육체적 고통과 정신적 고통을 모두 통틀어 일컫는 '고통'.
smell: 영화관에 진동하는 막 튀긴 팝콘 냄새. 달콤한 냄새라고 했으므로 아마 캐러멜 팝콘
   인 듯하다. 극빈자였던 주인공 소년은 냄새의 정체를 알지 못한다.

이런 하드보일드 스타일의 이야기는 단어를 최소한으로 한정하므로 여러 번 반복해서 읽고, 생략된 부분을 상상하면서 조금씩 보충해나가려는 노력이 필요합니다. 영어는 원래 우리말보다 객관적이므로 화자의 감정이 잘 드러나지 않습니다. 따라서 이야기 속에서 심각한 사건이 발생해도 한 발 물러나서 이상하리만큼 냉정한 내레이션을 곁들이기 때문에 음침하면서도 독특한 분위기를 자아냅니다. 이런 스타일의 내레이션은 우리말로는 좀처럼 표현하기 어려우므로 이번 기회에 영어만의 리듬감을 즐길 수 있기를 바라는 마음으로 수록했습니다.
그러니 영어의 또 다른 재미를 맛볼 수 있었으면 합니다. 그러나 취향에 따라 선호도가 달라질 수도 있는 문장과 내용이므로 잘 이해되지 않아도 크게 신경 쓸 필요는 없습니다. 영어에 다양한 문체가 있음을 깨달은 것만으로도 충분합니다.

BFC EXTRA SPECIAL
파이 콘테스트 참가자 명단

파이 페스티벌이 에버빌에서 열립니다!
파이라면 사족을 못 쓰는 사람도
파이가 별로인 사람도
모두 뉴 몰로 집합!

3:00P.M.

ALL NATURAL
NO PRESERVATIVES

STATE PIE

Welcome, folks, to the annual State Pie Festival! competing for the ultimate dream award for all pie you can purchase and take home your favorite pie PIEGAMES is sponsored by the New Everville Mall

FRUIT IN A CRUST
The only real fruit pie in the state

SUGAR & SPICE

Serving Excellent Chinese Cuisine To The Spyglass County For Twenty Five Years

BIG FAT CAT'S

3 COLOR

DICTI🐱NARY

BIG FAT CAT
vs.
MR. JONES

빅팻캣의 3색사전

~미스터 존스 편~

3색사전 사용법

녹색은 →, ⤴ 또는 =   진한 파란색은 두 번째 B′ 상자
                              (거의 나오지 않지만)

빨간색은 A 상자 | 파란색은 B 상자 | 색깔이 없는 부분은 부록

그래서 이런 문장 형태가 됩니다.

Ed gave the cat a present yesterday.   A→B=B′

일부 이해하기 어려운 문장은 바로 밑에 짧게나마 자세한 해설을 달아두었습니다.

3색사전은 스토리 부분의 영어 문장을 색깔로 구분하여 문장 형태를 한눈에 알아볼 수 있도록 만든 힌트북입니다. 물론 '정답'은 아닙니다. 영어 문장을 이해하기 위한 하나의 길잡이로 이용해주세요.

"George..."   불완전한 문장

"George..."   불완전한 문장

"It's morning."   A=B

p.9

"Oh... Ed. Good morning," George said.   A→B

p.10

He rubbed his sleepy eye with one hand as he got up.   A→B

두 문장이 as로 연결된 형태는 매우 자주 나옵니다. as 이하 두 번째 문장은 본래 동시에 일어난 일을 나타내는 '시간'의 부록이에요. 그러나 부록의 개념이 아니라 단순히 동시에 일어난 두 문장으로 이해해도 상관없습니다. 3색사전에서는 어려운 문장에 한해 별도의 두 문장으로 보고 색깔로 구분했어요.

The sun was barely up in the sky.   A=B

barely와 almost는 서로 의미가 비슷한 단어입니다. almost는 '조금 부족한 상태'고, barely는 '조금 넘친 상태'를 가리켜요. 여기서 barely는 해가 지평선을 지나 약간 떠오른 상태를 말해요.

Fresh and crisp air filled the dawn of Everville's older streets.   A→B

It was seven o'clock in the morning — the beginning of a new day.   A=B

After a moment of recovery, George smiled and pointed before him.

　　　A↻ and (A)→B

"There's your stuff.   A=B

stuff는 갖가지 사물을 포괄적으로 표현할 때 쓰는 편리한 단어입니다. 의미가 비슷한 또 다른 단어로 things도 있는데 20쪽의 두 번째 문장에 나와요.

Good and ready."   불완전한 문장

In front of George, there was a pile of kitchen utensils that Ed used everyday.   A=B

p.11

They were the cheapest brand at the nearby supermarket,

but now they shined like silver in the morning light.   A=B, but A⌐

cheap은 단순히 '싸다'는 의미보다는 '싼 게 비지떡'이란 부정적 이미지가 있는 단어입
니다. nearby는 '근처의'란 의미입니다.

Ed noticed that George's hands were all red.   A→B

**"This was all I could do. But I'll be in the front row today, cheering like
hell," George said.**   A→B

all I could do는 '내가 할 수 있는 모든 것'이란 뜻이에요.

Ed picked up his rolling pin.   A→B

Yesterday, it had been an old gray color.   A=B

Now it was practically new.   A=B

"George... we don't have any sandpaper.   A→B

This is impossible.   A=B

How did you..."   불완전한 문장

George took out a completely worn-out toothbrush.   A→B

He grinned like a child.   A⌐

Ed stood amazed.   A⌐

**He couldn't imagine how many hours it would take to scrub a rolling pin
with a toothbrush.**   A→B

to scrub 이하를 하는 데 조지가 들인 시간이 얼마인지 imagine할 수도 없었다는 뜻이
에요.

"George, this is impossible!"   A=B

"Almost," George said and smiled.   A→B and (A)⌐

'조금 부족한 상태'를 나타내는 almost입니다. '거의 불가능했지만 해냈지!'라는 의미로
조지가 의기양양하게 말하네요.

p.12 **Ed touched the rolling pin with the tip of his fingers.**   A→B

He thought he could feel the warmth inside.   A→B
> rolling pin의 inside를 말합니다.

"George, you can't sit in the front row today," he said to George.   A→B
> 오늘 열리는 파이 콘테스트 현장에서 벌어질 일에 대해 이야기를 나누고 있습니다.

"Oh..."   불완전한 문장

A look of despair crossed George's face for a moment.   A→B

But he replied quickly.   A↺

He was used to this kind of treatment all his life.   A=B
> 조지에게 익숙한 this kind of treatment는 에드가 조지에게 순간적으로 차갑게 대한 태도를 가리켜요.

"Oh... well, I know.   A↺

I guess I would make a bad impression on the judges.   A→B
> 노숙자로 보이는 사람이 제일 앞줄에서 like hell하게 응원했다간 아무래도 심사위원에게 좋은 인상을 주기는 힘들겠죠.

Hey, no problem!   불완전한 문장

I'll just stay in the back and keep..."   A↺ and (A)↺

Ed held the contest flier out to George.   A→B

An entry form and a list of rules were printed on the back.   A=B
> 이 문장에서의 back은 전단지 '뒷면'이에요.

Ed pointed to one particular rule.   A→B

"It says here, I can bring one assistant."   A→B   p.13
> It은 전단지의 대역입니다. 이 문장에서의 say는 '적혀 있다'란 의미예요.

Ed smiled.   A↺

"You're going to be that assistant."   A=B

"Say what?" George replied.   A→B

본래의 문장은 'What did you say?'로 다소 격의 없는 표현입니다.

His face turned red as he looked up at Ed.   A↺

turn은 순간적으로 상황이 급변할 때 사용하는 화살표입니다.

He immediately **shook his head.**   A→B

"**No way, man.**   불완전한 문장

No way는 관용구로 '그런 길(내가 조수가 되는 길) 따위는 없어', 다시 말해 '그런 일은 있을 수 없어'란 의미예요.

You don't want me!   A→B

Uh-un!   불완전한 문장

I'll just mess things up.   A→B

I always do."   A↺

do는 앞 문장의 화살표 mess의 대역입니다. mess의 정확한 뉘앙스는 '엉망진창으로 만들다'이에요.

"**I went to the Mall yesterday and registered. You already are my assistant, George. I need your help,**" **Ed said.**   A→B

George stared at Ed.   A→B

The morning sun, now higher in the sky, **gave bright light** onto the old neighborhood.   A→B

Most of the others were still asleep and **the street was quiet.**   A=B and A=B

"**Are you sure?**" **George asked.**   A→B

Ed nodded.   A↺

"**Nobody ever asked for my help. Ed... you're... you're so...**" **George said** in a trembling voice.   A→B

shake도 tremble도 '떨다'란 의미지만 tramble이 더 가늘게 떠는 모양이에요.

"**Come on, George,**" **Ed said,** looking up into the blue sky.   A→B

It seemed to be the start of a really nice winter day.   A=B

"**Let's get going.**"   (A)→B

Let's는 Let us의 줄임형이지만, '~하자'란 의미의 화살표로 생각해도 상관없습니다.
get going은 'going(가는 동작)을 취하다', 즉 '출발하다'라는 의미로 자주 사용하는 표현입니다.

"You're damn right, we're going!" George shouted as he stood up in pride.
A→B

And with that, the day began. A↺

that은 이 장면 전체를 가리키지만, 방금 전에 나온 조지의 대화문으로 파악해도 상관없습니다.

"AAAAND IT'S A GREAT NEW DAY!! A=B　　　p.14

단어를 길게 늘어뜨리며 발음할 때 영문에서는 이런 표기법을 사용하는 경우가 있어요.

The balloons are up! A=B

We're on top of the New Everville Mall this morning,
reporting live from the annual State Pie Festival! A=B

top은 Mall의 top, 즉 '뉴 에버빌 몰의 상공'이에요. 동시에 정신적인 고양감도 나타내요.

This is Glen Hamperton, bringing you the excitement below — live on the
morning news!" A=B

Today, eighteen shops and individuals enter the pie contest to find the best　　p.16
pie in the state. A→B

This year's main sponsor Wilson Artwill, the owner of the New Everville
Mall, has prepared a huge cash prize of twenty thousand dollars and a
free space for a shop in his Food Court. A→B

The rules are simple. A=B

Contestants have two hours to bake the best pie. A→B

to 이하는 2시간 동안 할 일을 구체적으로 설명해요.

They can use any ingredients they choose, but each contestant can have only one assistant for help.　A→B, but A→B

p.17

At the end of two hours, all the pies will be presented to the judges.　A=B

Each contestant will introduce their pie in the way they wish.　A→B
　　in 이하는 '어떻게'에 해당하는 부록이지만, 어떤 의미에서는 '장소'의 부록이기도 해요. '바라는 길 중에서' 다시 말해 '원하는 방식으로'란 의미지요.

After tasting all eighteen pies, the judges will each vote for the best pie.
　　A→B

The numbers will be added up, and the single contestant with the highest score will win the 'GOLDEN CRUST' trophy along with the prize money and the store space!　A=B and A→B
　　여기서의 numbers는 '득표수'입니다.

The excitement is heating up as the time draws near for the battle of the pies to begin!　A=B as A⤸

"WELCOME TO THE PIEGAMES!"　불완전한 문장
　　PIEGAMES는 이 대회를 위해 만들어진 신조어입니다. game은 '경쟁'이 있는 놀이에 전반적으로 사용되지만, 진지한 경기를 다소 유머러스하게 일컬을 때 사용되기도 해요.

"I'm Glen Hamperton reporting live from the air above Everville!　A=B

See you later, folks!"　(A)→B
　　folks라는 호칭은 군중을 상대로 친근하게 말을 건넬 때 사용해요.

p.18

The street was still quiet.　A=B

It was nearly nine a.m., but in Ghost Avenue, morning was longer than any other place.　A=B, but A=B

Ed crept through the piles of junk inside the Old Everville Cinema, heading towards the campfire in the middle.   A⤸

BeeJees was half-asleep **near the fire.**   A=B
어떤 단어에 half가 붙으면 대부분 효력을 약간 잃게 돼요. 딱 절반이 아니라 '대충 절반'으로 상당히 애매한 표현입니다. 여기서는 '선잠을 자고 있었다'라는 뜻이에요.

Besides him, Willy lay on a fake bed that Ed and the others had made.   A⤸
that 이하는 bed를 꾸미는 화장문입니다.

Willy hadn't woken up once in two days.   A⤸
부정문입니다. 4권의 마지막 장면에서 2일이 지났어요.

He was still alive, but barely.   A=B
다시 barely가 등장했네요. 삶과 죽음의 기로에서 생명이 '꺼져가는' 윌리의 상태를 나타내요.

"Willy," Ed whispered.   A→B

But Willy didn't react.   A⤸

"I have to go. But I'll be back soon. Then we'll get you to a hospital, okay?" Ed said.   A→B
you는 윌리의 대역입니다. '윌리를 가지고, 병원까지' 다시 말해 '윌리를 병원에 데리고 가다'란 의미이지요.

The light of the fire fell on Willy's face.   A⤸

Sometimes the flickering light made Willy seem to move a little.   A→B=B'
seem to가 붙어 있으므로 move a little한 것처럼 보였다는 의미입니다.

Unfortunately, it was always only a trick of the eye.   A=B

A faint cracking sound broke the silence.   A→B p.19

Ed looked behind him and found BeeJees awake, slumped against an old sign.   A⤸ and (A)→B=B'
awake 이하는 비지스의 상태입니다.

BeeJees was holding a fortune cookie which he had just cracked open in his

hands.   A=B

fortune cookie는 미국이나 캐나다의 중국 음식점에서 나오는 바싹 구운 쿠키로, 그 안에 그날의 운세가 적힌 쪽지가 담겨 있습니다(20쪽 삽화 참조). which 이하는 cookie를 꾸며주는 화장문이에요.

"BeeJees, I'm sorry about what I said the other night," Ed said to BeeJees.

A→B   the other night은 '(오늘이 아닌) 다른 날 저녁' 다시 말해 '며칠 전 저녁'입니다. 4권에 나왔던 병원으로 출발하기 직전에 에드가 한 말을 지금 사과하고 있네요.

"I... I'm really sorry."   A=B

BeeJees scratched his head, frowned, and looked down.

A→B, (A)↺, and (A)↺

He pulled out a thin piece of paper from inside the fortune cookie.   A→B

After a long pause, he read from the paper in a flat voice.   A→B

"There are chances, and there are consequences."   A=B, and A=B

consequence는 '결과' 중에서도 '부정적인 결과'에 치우친 느낌입니다. 중립적인 결과는 result예요.

BeeJees shook his head and chuckled.   A→B and (A)↺

chuckle은 해설 61쪽에 나온 '웃음'의 한 종류로 '쿡쿡'거리며 소리를 내지 않는 웃음을 나타내요.

"What the hell does that mean?"   A→B

p.20

He dropped the paper and cookie on the floor and crushed them under his foot.   A→B and (A)→B

"The Prof loved these things.   A→B

these things는 포춘 쿠키의 대역입니다. things란 단어는 뭐든지 '물건'으로 일괄해서 표현하므로 다소 얼버무리는 느낌이 있어요. 비지스도 '이런 종류의 것들을'이란 뉘앙스로 한 말이에요.

The Chinese store downtown used to give him cookies that had expired.

A→B / B'   used to는 그리운 과거를 회상할 때 씁니다. that 이하는 cookies를 꾸며

주는 화장문이에요.

He cracked one open every morning and **read the paper inside.**
A→B=B' and (A)→B

It always **said something stupid like that.**   A→B
that은 비지스가 방금 전에 읽은 운세입니다.

He just **read them and smiled.**   A→B and (A)↺

That crazy old bastard."   불완전한 문장
bastard는 원래 '못된 인간'이라는 의미로 쓰이는 욕입니다. 수줍음이 많은 비지스가 윌리에게 애정을 담아 역설적으로 표현한 것이에요. old는 단순히 '늙은'이란 의미가 아니라 왠지 '사랑할 수밖에 없는 노인네'라는 뜻으로 쓰였어요.

BeeJees laughed weakly.   A↺

Ed had taken his bandanna out and **was folding it in half.**   A→B and (A)=B

He wrapped it around his head and **tied it in the back.**   A→B and (A)→B

Right then, **Frank came** rolling around the corner in his toy wagon.   A↺
Right then은 '바로 그때'란 뜻이에요.

He said "Howdy" to Ed and **waved at him.**   A→B and (A)↺

Ed waved back.   A↺

"You really think you can win this contest?" **BeeJees asked.**   A→B

Ed held a solemn expression on his face, but **his eyes were determined.**
A→B, but A=B

BeeJees cracked open another fortune cookie.   A→B=B'

This time, **he crushed it** without even reading the paper inside.   A→B

"Do you at least **have a plan?**   A→B

Everyone else in the contest is a professional.   A=B

You're just a guy from a small town.   A=B

What do you plan to do?"   A→B

"What Willy told me."   불완전한 문장

Ed reached for his bag as he said, "Try to be a baker."   A→B
완전한 문장으로 쓰면 I will try to be a baker가 돼요.

p.21

Ed started for the door, looking back at Willy one last time.   A⤸

Willy slept on, cuddled in a pile of dirty rags.   A⤸
on은 무언가에 접촉해 있는 상태입니다. '자는 행위'에 접촉한 상태이므로 다시 말해 '계속 잠들어 있다'가 돼요.

At least he deserves a better bed, **Ed thought.**   A→B

It made him want to cry.   A→B=B'
It은 앞 문장 전체의 대역입니다.

But **there was no time** for crying.   A=B

"Watch the cat for me, Frank. It's going to be a disaster if the cat finds out where I'm going," **Ed said** to Frank.   A→B
if 이하는 '가능성'을 나타내는 문장입니다. 만약 if 이하가 일어나면 마치 '큰 재앙'이라도 닥칠 듯 에드가 우려하네요.

"Ai-ya!" **Frank replied.**   A→B

George was waiting by the doors, dressed in his best outfit.   A=B

It was a cheap tuxedo.   A=B

He looked like a boy waiting for his first day of Sunday school.   A=B
Sunday school은 아이들이 일요일이면 가는 '교회 주일학교'입니다. 대개 가장 단정한 옷을 입고 가지만, 정장은 너무 빼입은 느낌이므로 오히려 이상하게 보여요.

This made Ed smile again.   A→B=B'
This는 앞 문장 전체의 대역입니다.

"Ed," **BeeJees suddenly shouted.**   A→B

Ed looked back as BeeJees threw him a fortune cookie.   A⤸ as A→B/B'
as의 앞 문장과 뒤 문장은 거의 동시에 일어났어요.

Ed caught the cookie with both hands.   A→B

"Take Willy with you," BeeJees said.   A→B
> 결코 윌리 본인을 데려갈 수는 없으므로, 대신 포춘 쿠키를 가져가라는 의미입니다.

Ed raised his eyes and nodded once.   A→B and (A)↰

It was time to go.   A=B
> 'go할 시간' 다시 말해 '출발할 시간'이란 의미입니다.

"This is Glen Hamperton, reporting from outside the main tent of the State   `p.22`
Pie Festival.   A=B

The time is now ten a.m. and contestants should be here any minute now...
and YES!   A=B and A=B
> any minute은 '언제나'란 시간의 부록입니다.

Here they come!   A↰

This year's pie warriors!   불완전한 문장

"Leading the group is the two-time contest winner 'Brown Butters' — now
at four locations around the state.   A=B
> A 상자의 핵심을 The leader of the group으로 하면 이해하기 쉽습니다. 여기서의 time
> 은 '횟수'를 나타내는 time이에요.

Their famous 'Brown Butter Vanilla Double Crust' has been the number
one best-selling pie for more than fifteen years!   A=B

"Right behind them are the 'Buffi Brothers.'   A=B   `p.23`
> them은 Brown Butters(의 스태프들)를 가리키는 대역이에요.

Combining traditional Italian cuisine with the art of pie baking, they have
created a revolution in the history of pies.   A→B

Their specialty is the 'Pepperoni Pie' with cheese, tomato sauce, pasta and a whole lot of sliced pepperoni!   A=B

p.24

"And... oh my God... what is that blue smoke back there!?   A=B

Has there been an accident?   A=B

No, wait... that music, that rhythm... Yes, everyone!   불완전한 문장

This is the one you've been waiting for!   A=B
　　the one은 본래 the one pie shop입니다. you've 이하는 the one을 꾸며주는 화장문으로, 'the one의 정체가 무엇인지는…… 곧 알 수 있다'란 뜻이에요.

The crowd is going crazy!   A=B
　　'미쳤다'란 부정적인 의미로 쓰이던 crazy가, 현대 미국에서는 '미칠 듯이 굉장하다'란 의미로 쓰여, 오히려 칭찬하는 이미지가 강해졌습니다. 여기서도 '미칠 듯이 기뻐하다'로, 긍정적인 이미지를 나타내요.

We now present you, the one and only... ZOMBIE PIES!!   A→B / B'

p.25

"It's the strangest pie shop in the history of strange pie shops!   A=B

The Pie God himself, Jeremy Lightfoot Jr., and the colorful Zombie Pies trailer are now entering the tent.   A=B

Their horrifying mascot, 'The Gravedigger,' stalks the grounds while the 'Grim Zombies' are scaring kids who unfortunately got in their way!
　　A→B   grounds는 '지면'이지만 이 문장에서는 '일대'를 가리킵니다. who 이하는 kids를 꾸며주는 화장문이지만 어려우면 건너뛰어도 상관없어요. their way는 'Zombies가 지나가는 길'을 말해요.

Already condemned by twenty-one school boards, Zombie Pies is nevertheless the most famous pie shop in ten surrounding states!
　　A=B

"Reporting live from the entrance of the PIEGAMES, I'm Glen Hamperton!

A=B

The battle is about to begin!!"   A=B

Meanwhile... at the main gate.   불완전한 문장   p.26

"Oh my God..." George said, and forgot to shut his mouth.   A→B and (A)→B

"Ed, I think this is a big mistake."   A→B

    this는 '에드 일행이 콘테스트에 나가는 일'을 가리키는 대역입니다.

George stared at the fabulous Zombie Pies trailer truck as it entered the tent, his mouth wide open.   A→B

Ed was also frozen there at the gate of the pie festival.   A=B

    frozen은 '얼어붙은 듯한 상태'를 나타내요.

He scanned the festival grounds with both his eyes, surprised at how big the event was.   A→B

There was a Ferris wheel standing at the far side, along with several other carnival rides.   A=B

    에드와 조지가 서 있는 문에서 봤을 때 far side에 회전관람차가 있습니다. far라는 단어에서 대회장의 규모를 느껴보세요.

Countless booths selling every kind of pie on earth were lined back to back down the main area.   A=B   p.27

    selling에서 earth까지는 booths를 꾸며주는 화장품으로 '지구상에서 파는 모든 종류의 파이를 팔고 있다'라고 과장한 표현이고, back to back은 '등을 맞대고'란 뜻이에요.

People of all ages were everywhere.   A=B

    all ages는 '모든 연령'입니다.

There were balloons, flags, and other multi-colored decorations all around.

    A=B

Before arriving at the festival grounds, Ed had imagined an auditorium with
   fifty or a hundred people.   A→B
에드가 상상했던 대회장과는 상당히 다른 모습인 듯합니다.

He couldn't have been more wrong.   A=B
다소 모순된 표현을 쓴 언어유희의 표현입니다. '이 이상 틀리는 것은 불가능할 만큼 틀렸다'란 말로 에드의 짐작이 엄청난 착각이었음을 강조해요.

Ed gulped.   A↻

p.28

George looked at Ed with big, frightened-puppy eyes.   A→B

George was probably the only person in the whole festival grounds wearing
   a tuxedo, except for the stuffed bear on the counter of a nearby booth.
   A=B   조지와 같은 옷차림을 한 것은……. 26쪽의 삽화를 참고하세요.

"This is crazy, man.   A=B

BeeJees is right.   A=B

We're waaaay out of our league here.   A=B
waaaay는 물론 잘못 인쇄된 것이 아니에요. 이 문장에서 way는 away를 축약한 형태로 '훨씬 멀리'란 의미입니다. 너무 멀리 와 있음을 강조하기 위해 조지가 길게 발음하고 있습니다.

Let's go home."   (A)↻

George turned to leave, but Ed grabbed his arm.   A↻, but A→B

"George, we've got no choice."   A→B
no choice는 '선택권이 없다'는 뜻이에요.

"I know, man.   A↻

But I'm scared."   A=B

"Me too," Ed said, and started walking towards the main tent.
   A→B, and (A)→B

George stood there alone at the gate for a moment.   A↺

But when people nearby began to look at him suspiciously, he started to run after Ed — but fell because of his shaking legs.   A→B but (A)↺

He got up and continued to run.   A↺ and (A)→B

"Ed!   불완전한 문장

Hey!   불완전한 문장

Wait up!   (A)↺

Ed!"   불완전한 문장

Unnoticed by either of them, a dark shadow crouched by the gate silently, watching everything.   A↺
them은 에드와 조지의 대역입니다.

"Thank you, Glen.   (A)→B

p.29

TV 리포터가 콘테스트의 사회자로 바뀌자 중계 장소도 텐트 안으로 바뀌었어요.

And now, this is your host Robert R. Silverman from inside the main tent.
A=B

Almost all of the contestants have finished setting up their kitchens here on the battleground.   A→B

All we can do is wait for the clock to... oops, someone just came into the tent from the contestant's side."   A=B, A↺
에드가 someone으로 표현된 이유는 전혀 콘테스트의 참가자로는 보이지 않았기 때문입니다.

"Hey, mister, you've got the wrong gate!   A→B
사회자는 에드 일행을 손님으로 착각하고 있습니다.

But, oh... wait a minute... am I dreaming this, or...   (A)→B... A=B

Good Lord!   불완전한 문장

This man seems to be our last contestant!" A=B

seems만이 아니라 seems to be까지 모두 등호로 생각하면 이해하기 쉬워요.

"He has now stopped at booth five. A⊃

He는 에드의 대역입니다.

Let's see... his name seems to be 'Ed Wishbone.' A=B

Let us see의 줄임형이에요. 말 그대로 '보자'란 의미지만, '어디 좀 볼까'라는 느낌으로 말을 꺼낼 때 쓰는 관용구입니다.

Funny, the name sort of rings a bell. A→B

이 문장에서의 Funny는 고개를 갸우뚱하게 할 만큼 '이상하다'는 의미입니다.

Where have I heard... A⊃

Holy cow! 불완전한 문장

It's the baker from Ghost Avenue! A=B

We've all seen him on the six o'clock news! A→B

My God, I don't want to be rude here, but Ed, man, maybe you should open your eyes and take a look around!" A→B, but A→B and (A)→B

p.30

"Uh-oh... More bad news. 불완전한 문장

I'm afraid Mr. Tuxedo here is Ed's assistant. A=B (that) A=B

I just hope that barrel he's dragging isn't what I think it is. A→B

that 이하의 문장은 isn't가 등호이고 isn't 양쪽이 각각 A 상자, B 상자에 해당합니다. what I think it is란 문장은 '내가 생각한 그것'. '설마 그것이 오븐은 아니겠지'라고 사회자는 hope하고 있어요.

If this is a joke, it sure seems to work, because everyone in the stands is laughing like crazy. A=B

드럼통이 웃음을 유발하기 위한 것이라면 성공했다는 뜻입니다. 여기에서의 crazy도 긍정적인 이미지로 쓰였어요.

Ladies and gentlemen, let's just hope that the judges' health is still intact when they go home tonight!"   (A)→B

hope하고 있는 내용은 that 이하입니다.

"Holy macaroni! Is that his oven!?" Jeremy's assistant said.   A→B

p.31

He was laughing and pointing at Ed as they set up the barrel oven.   A=B

George was so embarrassed that he lost his grip, and the barrel oven
toppled over.   A=B that A→B, A↺

grip을 잃다' 다시 말해 '꽉 쥐고 있던 주먹을 펴다'란 뜻이에요. '당연히 쥐고 있던 오븐
이 toppled하고 말았다'란 의미입니다.

The crowd went wild.   A↺

이 문장에서의 wild도 crazy와 엇비슷한 의미로 쓰였습니다. wild는 본래 '야성적'이란
의미였지만 일상에서 사용할 때는 '야생이나 다름없이' 즉 '마구'란 의미로 주로 쓰여요.
보통은 crazy보다 더 격렬한 상태를 나타냅니다.

Ed and George just kept on trying to balance the barrel.   A→B

The crowd laughed as if they were watching a circus.   A↺

as if 이하는 '마치 ~한 듯이'로 비유적인 표현입니다.

"Is he really going to enter the contest!?   A=B

Man, talk about crazy people..."   (A)→B

이 문장도 자주 쓰이는 표현으로, 생략하지 않고 쓰면 'Man, we talk about crazy
people, but he sure is one'이에요. 'crazy한 사람이 있다고는 하지만'이란 의미로 놀
란 느낌을 드러냈어요. 이 문장에서의 crazy가 긍정적인지 부정적인지는 해석하기 나름
이에요.

"Shut up," Jeremy said.   A→B

He was concentrating on checking the oven.   A=B

"But boss, you should take a look at this guy.   A→B

He is totally out of his..."   A=B

Jeremy hit the top of the oven hard with his hand.   A→B

The assistant stopped babbling.   A→B

Jeremy was dressed in costume, but his face was dead serious.
 A=B, but A=B

He slowly pulled his hand back and hid it behind him.
 A→B and (A)→B

It hurt.   A↺

"I said... quiet.   A→B

Stop laughing, and keep your mind on your job."   (A)→B, and (A)→B=B'
 '정신을 일에 붙들어두어라' 다시 말해 '일에 집중하라'란 뜻이지요.

The surprised assistant replied, "Yes, sir."   A→B
 surprised는 조수를 꾸며주는 화장품입니다. 조수는 평소와는 다른 제레미 때문에 당혹
 스런 기색이네요.

He got back to work in a hurry.   A↺

Jeremy glanced at Ed and George with a look of disgust, then focused again
 on his oven.   A→B, then (A)→B
 with에서 쉼표까지는 '어떻게'의 부록입니다.

He tried to dismiss the duo from his mind, but kept remembering the taste
 of that pie.   A→B, but (A)→B
 the duo는 에드와 조지의 대역으로 '2인조'를 가리켜요. that pie는 에드가 만든 파이,
 제레미가 4권에서 뒤집어썼던 그 파이를 말합니다.

An ordinary pie.   불완전한 문장

That was all.   A=B

An ordinary fruit pie.   불완전한 문장

But he still couldn't forget the taste.   A→B

It made him nervous.   A→B=B'

"Okay, Wishbone. You're here," Jeremy mumbled.   A→B

"Now, prove yourself." (A)→B
전에도 제레미가 에드에게 말했던 대화문입니다. 드디어 에드가 '자신을 증명할 때'가 왔
네요.

Meanwhile behind the Zombie Pies trailer. 불완전한 문장 p.33

Billy Bob listened to his cell phone in silence. A→B
cellular phone의 축약으로, 휴대전화를 영어로 말할 때 일상적으로 쓰는 표현입니다.

He didn't say anything. A→B

He didn't even nod. A↺

He just listened. A↺

Finally, before hanging up, he said one phrase. A→B

"Yes, sir." 불완전한 문장

**Billy Bob was standing between the trailer and the back wall where almost
nobody could see him.** A=B
where 이하는 '장소'의 부록으로 빌리 밥이 현재 있는 곳의 상황을 설명합니다.

**He carefully set Mr. Jones' carrier cage down on the ground and moved
away into the back alley.** A→B and (A)↺

A moment later, Jeremy's assistant came rushing out of the trailer.
A↺

Jeremy was yelling, "Go get it and hurry!" from behind him. A=B
it이 무엇의 대역인지는 불분명하지만 파이에 사용되는 것임에는 틀림없습니다. him은
달려가는 조수를 가리키는 대역이에요.

**The assistant was so upset that he swung open the back door with all of his
might.** A=B that A→B
with 이하는 '어떻게'의 부록으로 '온 힘을 다해'란 의미로 쓰인 표현입니다.

The door hit Mr. Jones' cage and knocked it over. A→B and (A)→B
it은 Mr. Jones' cage를 가리키는 대역이에요.

p.34

The carrier rolled over twice and the door of the cage sprang wide open.
A↺ and A↺

Everything lay still for a while.   A↺
이해하기 어려우면 lay를 was로 바꿔서 읽어보세요. 여기서의 still은 '조용한'이란 뜻이
에요.

But then, inch by inch, Mr. Jones pushed its head out and looked around.
A→B and (A)→B   inch by inch는 '1인치씩', 즉 '아주 조금씩'이란 의미를 나타내요.

— After a brief pause, Mr. Jones hid inside the cage again.   A↺

Another minute passed.   A↺

Mr. Jones decided to take a step outside again.   A→B

It slowly crept out of the cage, and even more slowly, took one step, then
two steps out on the ground.   A↺, and (A)→B

It felt good.   A↺
여기서의 It은 지금의 상황 전체를 가리키는 대역이지만, Mr. Jones의 대역으로 볼 수도
있어요.

Mr. Jones took a big stretch and narrowed its eyes.   A→B and (A)→B

It then walked over to a trailer tire, sniffed it, and rubbed a side against it.
A↺, (A)→B, and (A)→B

Satisfied, Mr. Jones continued walking down the alley.   A→B

It couldn't understand what was happening, but being outside of the cage
was much better than being inside of it.   A→B, but A=B
첫머리의 It은 Mr. Jones의 대역이고, 마지막의 it은 애완동물 가방의 대역입니다. '가방
안'과 '가방 밖'을 비교하고 있어요.

Free space to walk around was luxurious.   A=B
Mr. Jones에게 멋진 것이라면 '자유롭게 거닐 수 있는 공간'이에요.

So this was the world outside.   A=B
So가 문두에 단독으로 나오면 '과연 그렇지'와 같은 뉘앙스를 풍겨요.

The world beyond the bars.   불완전한 문장

It was so free, and...   A=B

p.35

... and it was also pretty scary.   A=B

p.36

The last time George had seen a real Santa Claus was more than thirty years ago, back in elementary school.   A=B

p.37

The last time은 '(조지가 실제로 산타의 모습을 본) 마지막 때'입니다. real을 화장품으로 산타란 단어에 붙인 부분이 정말 조지다운 말투예요.

His mom had taken all the kids to the Outside Mall one afternoon, where Santa came every winter.   A→B

Back then, **the Outside Mall was the coolest place a kid could go.**   A=B

Back은 시간에 쓰일 때도 '뒤쪽' 즉 과거를 가리킵니다. cool이란 단어는 구어체에서 모든 연령, 성별, 인종을 초월하여 최상급에 속하는 칭찬으로 '멋지다'란 의미예요.

Now, thirty years later, **a chubby Santa with a white beard and red suit was walking** straight towards them.   A=B

"Ed Wishbone?" **Santa Claus asked.**   A→B

George turned to Ed, his eyes wide open.   A⤸

"You're friends with Santa?" **George asked.**   A→B

Ed looked up from the table as Santa took off his beard.   A⤸

얼굴에서 턱수염을 off하자 드러난 본모습은…….

It was the owner of the New Mall.   A=B

"Ed Wishbone! I thought that was you!" **the owner said.**   A→B

p.38

that은 오너가 멀리서 바라본 에드의 모습입니다.

"I was worried after you disappeared from the clinic. Are you okay?"
A=B

Ed smiled awkwardly as he replied.   Aↄ

"I'm fine, sir.   A=B

I'm sorry for everything.   A=B

I don't really remember much about that night."   A→B
that night은 2권 〈빅팻캣, 도시로 가다〉에서 일어난 어느 하룻밤의 일이에요.

"No problem, no problem," the owner said, but the smile faded from his
face.   A→B, but Aↄ

"You know, Jeremy Lightfoot's bodyguard came to my office several days
after you disappeared.   Aↄ
several 이하는 '시간'의 부록입니다.

He had a paper with your signature on it.   A→B

It said that you disclaimed all rights to the space in the Food Court.   A→B
It은 '에드가 강압에 의해서 서명한 종이'의 대역입니다.

I knew the paper was suspicious, but I really had no choice but to believe
it."   A→B, but A→B

Ed nodded.   Aↄ

"So I didn't rent the space to Zombie Pies, either.   A→B

Instead, I saved it as the prize for the contest today.   A→B=B'
it은 결국 오너가 누구의 손에도 넘기지 않았던 space in the Food Court의 대역입니다.
space는 최종적으로 as 이하와 같이 되었어요.

I sincerely hope you win."   A→B

p.39   "Thank you."   (A)→B

"I'm sorry about what happened."   A=B

118

"No. 불완전한 문장

Don't be. 불완전한 문장

두 문장 앞의 I'm sorry에 대해서 Don't be (sorry), 즉 '미안해하지 말라'고 말하고 있어요.

It was all for the best. A=B

'모든 것이 최선의 결과를 위해 작용하고 있다'란 매우 긍정적인 표현이에요.

I..." 불완전한 문장

Just then, a bell rang throughout the main tent, signaling the start of the contest in five minutes. A↻

in five minutes는 앞으로 5분 이내에(in) 콘테스트를 시작한다는 말이에요. 즉 '5분 후'를 뜻합니다.

The owner hurriedly put his beard back on. A→B

his face에 beard를 on했다는 뜻이에요.

He smiled at Ed. A↻

"Good luck, Mr. Wishbone." 불완전한 문장

"Thank you, sir," Ed said. A→B

The owner ran off, his fluffy cap flip-flopping with every step. A↻

"I didn't know Santa's beard was fake," George said in an astonished face.
A→B

Ed chuckled and turned back to his table. A↻ and (A)↻

Everything was ready and in place. A=B

in place는 '있어야 할 곳에 있다'는 의미입니다.

The only thing now was to decide what kind of pie to make. A=B

Ed knelt down and inspected the bags he had brought. A↻ and (A)→B p.40

he 이하는 bags를 꾸며주는 화장문입니다.

In one bag were the ingredients for a blueberry pie.   A=B

But the other bag held the ingredients for another kind of pie.   A→B

Ed had not mentioned this to George.   A→B
   this는 앞 문장의 내용을 가리키는 대역입니다.

The safe choice was blueberry.   A=B

There was no doubt about it.   A=B

Yet, something inside Ed kept telling him that he should enter the contest
   with his own pie.   A→B
   에드의 내면에 자리한 무언가가 that 이하의 생각을 속삭이고 있습니다.

Not a pie borrowed from his mother's recipe book.   불완전한 문장
   앞 문장의 his own을 좀 더 구체적으로 설명하고 있습니다. borrowed 이하는 pie를 꾸
   며주는 화장품이에요.

But that was risky.   A=B
   that은 두 문장 앞에 나왔던 '에드의 생각'에 따른 행동을 가리키는 대역이에요.

It was more than a risk.   A=B

Yet...   불완전한 문장

His hand was moving slowly towards the second bag when George said,
   A=B

"Damn!   불완전한 문장

Willy sure would have wanted to see this!"   A→B
   sure는 강조를 표현한 단어입니다. this는 '이 화려한 대회 무대'를 가리켜요.

p.41 Ed's hand stopped a few inches from the bag.   A↺

He clenched the hand into a fist, then grabbed the bag with the blueberries
   in it instead.   A→B, (A)→B

Willy.   불완전한 문장

Ed thought to himself.   A↩

Think about Willy.   (A)→B

You have to win.   A→B
'이길 것을 예정 중에 가지고 있다', 다시 말해 '이겨야만 한다'란 뜻이지요. 에드가 자신
에게 한 말이에요.

No matter what.   불완전한 문장
'무슨 일이 있어도'란 의미로 쓰이는 관용구입니다. what은 '일어날 수 있는 온갖 종류의
문제를 통틀어'란 의미로 쓰인 대역이에요. 이기기 위해서라면 어떤 문제도 no matter,
즉 상관없다는 뜻이에요.

Moments later, the bell rang again, and all of the contestants sprang to a
start.   A↩, and (A)↩
sprang은 sprang이 변형된 형태로 여기서 spring은 '봄'이 아니라 '용수철(스프링)'
이라는 의미로 쓰여 '(용수철처럼 빨리) ~하다'란 화살표로 쓰였어요.

The clock tower standing in the middle of the tent turned twelve.   A↩

The host was shouting in excitement.   A=B

The crowd roared.   A↩

And from there on, **everything became a blur.**   A=B
there는 물리적인 장소가 아니라 시간 개념으로 쓰였습니다. 즉 콘테스트가 시작된 시점
이에요.

The world seemed to move in fast-forward.   A=B

The battle had begun.   A↩

An hour later, **Jeremy was** about to finish **his crust** when he noticed Billy
   Bob standing near Ed Wishbone's booth.   A=B

p.42

Only Jeremy and a few others could have possibly **spotted him.**   A→B

He was standing in a shadowy corner.   A=B

A bad feeling ran through Jeremy's mind as **his busy hands stopped moving**

for a moment.   A↰ as A→B

Billy Bob was checking to see if Ed Wishbone and his assistant were away from their table.   A=B
checking to see는 '살펴보고 있다', if 이하 문장은 '가능성'을 나타내는 문장입니다. 즉 빌리 밥은 if 이하의 가능성을 살펴보고 있어요.

—They were.   A=(B)
They는 '에드와 조지'의 대역입니다. 강조하기 위해 도중에서 문장을 끝냈지만 뒤이어 앞 문장에 나왔던 away의 의미가 무엇인지 나와요. 구체적인 내용은 다음 문장에서 나 옵니다.

Ed and George were over by the barrel oven, trying to build up a steady fire.
A=B

Before Jeremy could even think, Billy Bob stepped out.   A↰

He took something from the table and replaced it with something else.
A→B and (A)→B

It was impossible to determine what it was, but he had definitely done something to Wishbone's materials.   A=B, but A→B
첫머리의 It은 to determine에서 쉼표까지의 대역이고, 두 번째 it은 빌리 밥이 슬쩍 바 꿔치기한 '것'을 가리키는 대역이에요.

p.43 **When Ed returned to his table a few seconds later, Billy Bob had disappeared completely, as if he had never been there.**   A↰
as if 이하는 일반 부정문처럼 보이지만, 빌리 밥이 실제로는 그 장소에 있었기 때문에 비 유적으로 쓰인 표현입니다. '마치 그 자리에 없었던 것처럼', 빌리 밥은 역시 행동이 재 빠르네요.

Jeremy took off his apron and laid it on the table.   A→B and (A)→B

He hurried out of the trailer and went racing through the back door.
A↰ and (A)↰

Billy Bob was just coming down the alley.   A=B

Enraged, Jeremy confronted Billy Bob head-on. A→B

"You! 불완전한 문장

What were you doing? A=B

Tell me!" (A)→B

Jeremy grabbed Billy Bob by his jacket and pulled, but Billy Bob didn't
  move an inch. A→B and (A)↺, but A↺

Nor did his expression change. A↺
  문장 전체가 부정문입니다. 고쳐서 쓰면 'His expression did not change, either'예요.

"Did my father tell you to do this?" A→B/B'
  this는 제레미가 목격한 빌리 밥의 '수상한 행동 전체'를 가리키는 대역입니다.

Billy Bob didn't answer. A↺

p.44

"Damn it! (A)→B

I'm not going to let you and my father mess this up! A=B
  let이란 화살표는 '허용하다'란 의미가 있습니다. 이 문장은 부정문이므로 you(빌리 밥)
  와 father(제레미의 아버지)가 바라는 바를 '허용할 수 없다'고 제레미가 말하고 있어요.

I'm going to win this on my own!" A=B
  on my own은 '자기 자신에게 기대어', 다시 말해 '나 혼자 힘으로'라는 의미를 지니는 관
  용구입니다.

Billy Bob's cell phone rang. A↺

With one movement, Billy Bob brushed Jeremy aside and pulled his phone
  out. A→B and (A)→B

Jeremy went sprawling to the ground, hitting his elbow hard. A↺

Ignoring Jeremy, Billy Bob answered the phone. A→B

Only Billy Bob's eyes kept watching Jeremy, as if Jeremy too was a pet.
  A→B too는 이해하기 어려우면 삭제하고 읽어도 돼요.

"It's done," Billy Bob said into the phone, then hung up.   A→B, then (A)↺

It이 무엇의 대역인지는 파악 못해도 상관없습니다. 어쨌든 빌리 밥이 에드의 물건에 손을 댄 것은 틀림없지만……

He walked away without any more words.   A↺

Jeremy closed his eyes in both anger and bitterness.   A→B

Back in the main arena, the host continued to feed the crowd's excitement.
   A→B

Upbeat music rocked the thin walls.   A→B

The noise all blended together, erasing all sound, including the voice of
   Jeremy crying.   A↺

p.45

"The clock now reads one-forty-five.   A→B

Only fifteen minutes left!   불완전한 문장

   정확하게 쓰면 'Only fifteen minutes are left'예요.

"Most of the pies are already in the oven.   A=B

There's a nice smell of sugar and spice in the air as I speak!   A=B

   이제 친숙해진 as 이하 문장은 동시에 일어난 일을 나타내는 '시간'의 부록입니다.

"Zombie Pies owner Jeremy Lightfoot Jr. disappeared mysteriously from
   his kitchen around the end of the first hour.   A↺

We have no information regarding Lightfoot's disappearance, but it may be
   part of some secret plan.   A→B, but A=B

   it은 Lightfoot's dis-appearance의 대역이에요.

"Meanwhile, Ed Wishbone and his assistant, now known to the audience
   as 'the Tux', have continued to hold the crowd's attention with their
   very unusual oven.   A→B

   now에서 Tux까지는 조수, 즉 조지를 꾸며주는 화장품입니다. 상황에 어울리지 않는 턱시도 차림을 The Tux라고 짧게 줄여서 놀리고 있어요.

"Oops, it seems for the moment, Ed has disappeared too.   A=B

But I think it's a safe guess that this has nothing to do with any secret plan."
   A→B   guess는 추측할 때 즐겨 쓰는 단어입니다. 우리말로 '~라고 생각한다'고 할 때 영어는 I guess라는 표현을 써요. 여기서는 사회자가 'safe(안전한) guess'라고 말했습니다. 즉 Ed's disappearance가 secret plan과 아무런 관계가 없는 것이 '맞을 확률이 높은 안전한 추측'이란 의미지요. 45쪽의 삽화를 보면 확실히 그런 것 같지만……

"Wishbone!"   불완전한 문장   p.46

Ed stopped in the middle of the back alley when he heard his name.   A↺

Jeremy had appeared out of the shadows behind him.   A↺

In this damp, dark corridor, all the music and excitement seemed far away, as if it came from a different world.   A=B
   또 '비유적 표현'인 as if가 나왔습니다. 음악 소리나 환호성이 저 멀리 있는 different world에서 들려오는 것처럼 느껴졌다는 말이에요.

Jeremy was alone.   A=B

He slowly took a few steps towards Ed.   A→B

Ed nervously took a step back.   A→B

Jeremy Lightfoot Jr. wore a solemn face.   A→B
   평소의 제레미에게서는 좀처럼 볼 수 없는 표정이었으므로 wore(몸에 걸치다)란 화살표를 쓴 거예요.

He closed his eyes for a moment, clenched his fists, and just stood there.
   A→B, (A)→B and (A)↺

He seemed like he was fighting something inside of himself.   A=B
   앞의 He와 뒤의 he는 모두 제레미를 가리켜요.

"I... uh... have to go," Ed said, and took a step back towards his booth as Jeremy opened his mouth.   A→B, and (A)→B

"Check your pie," Jeremy said.   A→B

p.47

"What?" Ed asked.   A→B

"Your pie.   불완전한 문장

I saw someone mess with your supplies when you weren't looking."

    A→B=B'   앞에서도 종종 나왔던 mess란 단어를 썼습니다. stuff, guess 등과 마찬가지로 구어체다운 애매한 표현이므로 언제나 사용할 수 있어서 편리해요.

Ed stared at Jeremy.   A→B

In the quiet refuge of the back alley, the two young bakers really saw each other for the first time.   A→B

And for some reason, it seemed like looking into a mirror.   A=B

    it은 앞 문장의 saw each other를 가리키는 대역이에요.

They both realized it was not a matter of money or pride or proving anything anymore.   A→B

    it은 현재 두 사람이 처한 상황을 가리키는 대역입니다. 이해하기 어려우면 바로 '싸우는 이유'로 바꿔서 생각해보세요. 하지만 애매모호하게 표현한 문장이 사실은 더 재미있지요.

It was just about pies now.   A=B

"My pie?" Ed whispered, his face clouding.   A→B

Jeremy nodded.   A↩

p.48

Ed glanced at the clock on the wall.   A→B

There were only thirteen more minutes until time was up.   A=B

If something was wrong with the pie he was baking now, there was no time to start over again.   A=B

    If에서 쉼표까지는 에드가 가능한 한 상상조차 하고 싶지 않은 무서운 추측입니다. 만약 그렇게 됐다면 no time이라고 에드는 생각하고 있어요.

"Go," Jeremy said.   A→B

Ed nodded.   A↩

He started to run back but paused briefly only to say to Jeremy, "Thanks."

A→B but (A)↶

Jeremy closed his eyes again as Ed went dashing for the door.　A→B as A↶

He couldn't tell Ed who had messed with his stuff, and it hurt.

A→B/B', and (A)↶

제레미는 에드의 재료를 바꿔치기한 인물(who)을 에드에게 밝힐 수 없었습니다. it은 말하지 못한 사실을 가리키는 대역이에요.

It hurt very badly.　A↶

여기서의 It도 범인의 정체를 밝히지 못한 사실을 가리키는 대역입니다.

Ghost Avenue.　불완전한 문장 p.49

Same time.　불완전한 문장

Frank hurled piles of rotting magazines and pieces of wood into the fire, trying to warm up the theater.　A→B

But it was still cold.　A=B

이 문장에서의 it은 기온을 나타내는 it입니다. '시간', '기온' 등 애매한 대상의 대역은 it에게 맡기세요.

The cruel coldness sneaked in through the hole in the roof, the cracks in the wall, the broken windows, and anywhere else it could.　A↶

through 이하는 모두 '장소'의 부록입니다. 마지막 문장에서 anywhere(어디든)라고 했지만 분위기를 연출하기 위해 구체적인 장소를 서술했어요.

Willy had started shaking a few minutes ago.　A→B

BeeJees brought every rag he could find and wrapped them around Willy but the shaking didn't subside.　A→B and (A)→B but (A)↶

he could find는 rag를 꾸며주는 화장문입니다.

"Frank! More fire! Burn everything! Anything!" BeeJees shouted frantically.　A→B

Frank immediately took off his jacket and threw it into the fire.

A→B and (A)→B

But it was no use.   A=B

it은 프랭크가 불에 던진 재킷을 가리키는 대역입니다. 그러나 '소용이 없었다' 다시 말해 '도움이 되지 못했다'란 뜻이에요.

p.50

"Prof!   불완전한 문장

Prof!   불완전한 문장

Hang on!   (A)↺

화살표 hang은 '매달리다', '붙들다'란 의미로 쓰이는 단어입니다. 윌리는 지금 생명의 끈을 간신히 부여잡고 있는 상태예요. hang on은 대표적인 관용구로, 우리말로는 '끝까지 버텨, 포기하지 마'라는 표현에 가까운 말이에요. 즉 '힘들어도 Hang on!(손을 놓지 마!)'이란 뜻이지요.

Stay with me, Prof!   (A)↺

That kid will be back soon with the money!   A=B

That kid는 에드이고, money는 물론 콘테스트에서 받는 상금을 말해요.

I know he will!   A→B

Just hold on!"   (A)↺

Willy kept shaking.   A→B

BeeJees, tears in his eyes, hugged Willy from top of the blankets, trying to keep him from falling off the bed.   A→B

BeeJees was scared.   A=B

He was so scared.   A=B

"Hurry, Ed!" BeeJees said.   A→B

It sounded like a prayer.   A↺

"Please hurry... Please..."   (A)↺

p.51

"George! 불완전한 문장

The oven! 불완전한 문장

Check the pies!" (A)→B

George looked towards the back door. A→B

He saw Ed come running back with a hint of panic in his eyes. A→B=B'

The pies would be done in maybe another five minutes. A=B
'파이가 done됐다'는 말은 '파이가 다 구워졌다'는 뜻이에요. another는 사실 an과 other가 합성된 단어입니다. another ten minutes는 '또 다른 10분', 다시 말해 '10분 후'이지요.

He couldn't understand why Ed was in such a rush. A→B

"Hey, man. 불완전한 문장

Take it easy. (A)→B
'편하게 받아들여' 다시 말해 '침착해'라는 의미로 쓰이는 관용구예요.

Everything's fine, man." A=B

Ed ran past George, grabbed the mitten hanging on the side of the oven, and without any hesitation, opened the oven door.
A↺, (A)→B, and (A)→B

A cloud of smoke rose out of the small door, making Ed and George cough.
A↺ making을 바로 이해하기 어려우면 the smoke made로 바꿔서 뒷부분을 별도의 문장으로 생각하고 읽어보세요.

Ed knew immediately that something was terribly wrong. A→B
Ed가 knew한 내용은 that 이하입니다.

There shouldn't be this much smoke inside the oven. A=B

He gulped as the smoke began to clear. A↺
as 이하는 '시간'의 부록으로 '연기가 clear해지기 시작했을 때'예요.

As soon as he could see inside, Ed pulled a slightly burned pie out of the oven and hurried over to the table. A→B and (A)↺

p.52

"Ed! What the hell are you doing!?" George shouted when he saw Ed take out a cutting knife.   A→B

"That pie isn't finished yet!"   A=B

But Ed cut the pie in half.   A→B

He broke off a piece of crust, dipped it in the filling, and popped it in his mouth.   A→B, (A)→B, and (A)→B

He tasted it for a moment and froze.   A→B and (A)↻
froze한 사람은 에드입니다.

Ed said something but the applause of the audience was getting louder and George couldn't hear him.   A→B but A=B and A→B

"...other pie," Ed said again to George, but most of it was drowned out by the sound of the audience.   A→B, but A=B
it은 방금 전에 한 에드의 대사지만 청중 소리에 파묻혀버렸네요.

"Say what?" George asked close to Ed's ear.   A→B

"Get the other pie out of the oven! Fast!" Ed repeated, much louder this time.   A→B
에드가 한 말치고는 상당히 어조가 강한 명령문입니다. 너무 절박한 상황이라 에드도 여유를 잃은 거예요.

p.53

Hearing the urgency in Ed's voice, George flew over to the oven and returned quickly with the other pie.   A↻ and (A)↻
lew라는 화살표는 쏜살같이 빠른 동작을 말해요. run이나 dash보다 훨씬 속도감이 있습니다.

Ed cut this one in half too, and tasted a piece of it.   A→B, and (A)→B

His reaction was almost the same.   A=B

But this time, his face lost color completely.   A→B

George also took a piece of the pie and bit into it.   A→B and (A)→B

Almost instantly, he spit it out.　A→B

"God!　불완전한 문장

What the hell...?"　불완전한 문장

George turned to Ed.　A↺

"Someone did something to my stuff," Ed said.　A→B

에드는 누군가 꾸민 일이라는 사실 외에는 아무것도 알 수 없었습니다. stuff도 의미가
불분명한 단어이므로 상당히 애매모호한 문장이지요.

George couldn't understand what Ed said for a moment.　A→B

Then, the full horror sank in.　A↺

이 순간이 오기 전까지는 무슨 일이 일어났는지 조지는 미처 몰랐던 모양입니다. 하지만
곧 공포가 온몸에 엄습해오는 상황을 sank라는 단어로 표현했어요.

The pies were ruined.　A=B

There was no more time left.　A=B

Ed glanced at the clock tower.　A→B

Seven minutes.　불완전한 문장

The contest was in full swing.　A=B

full swing은 휘두르는 반경이 최대치가 된 순간, 즉 절정에 다다른 상태를 말합니다. 전
속력으로 야구방망이를 휘둘러 공을 치는 순간에도 같은 표현을 써요.

Most of the contestants were carrying finished pies from their booths to the
　　judges' area.　A=B

Ed could do nothing except stare at the two ruined pies on the table.　A→B

이제 에드가 할 수 있는 일이라고는 except 이하의 행동 정도예요.

"Ed!"　불완전한 문장

p.54

George tugged on Ed's sleeve.　A→B

"C'mon, Ed!　A↺

We still have time!　A→B

I'll run and get anything!　A↺ and (A)→B

Just tell me what you need!"　A→B/B'

Ed still hadn't recovered control, but he said to George in a trembling voice.
　　A→B, but A↺

"Heat... two more cups of blueberry in a saucepan."　(A)→B
　　you가 생략된 명령문입니다.

"Gotcha!"　불완전한 문장

George dashed away, confident that Ed knew a way to repair the pie.　A↺
　　confident 이하는 George를 꾸며주는 화장문입니다. 이 문장에서 way는 '(수리하는)
　　길=방법'이에요.

But he didn't.　A↺
　　본래 문장은 But he didn't know입니다. 앞 문장의 내용을 받아서 '그렇지 않았다'고 부
　　정하고 있어요. 단 7분 만에 파이를 완성시키는 방법이 있을 리가 없기 때문이지요.

He had started scraping the filling out of the crust, but he knew it was
　　impossible.　A→B, but A→B

There was no way to make a pie in seven minutes.　A=B

5권을 끝내며

시리즈도 권을 맞이하여 한층 더 깊이 있는 내용으로 발전했습니다. 이번 작품의 〈BFC BOOKS PRESENTS〉에서는 문법이나 독해 요령과 같은 기본 학습 수준에서 더 나아가 언어의 본질적인 측면을 살펴봤습니다. 즉 언어의 신비한 힘과 언어가 가지는 애매모호함에 대해서 서술했지요. 영어 문장을 보자마자 'A→B'와 같이 기계적으로 읽어나가는 것을 걱정했기 때문입니다.

물론 언어에는 어느 정도 익혀야 할 문법과 일정한 규칙이 있습니다. 이런 부분은 옳고 그름을 따져서 채점할 수도 있습니다. 그러나 언어에는 문법만으로는 결코 설명할 수 없는 신비한 힘이 담겨 있습니다. 완벽하게 이해는 못해도 어쩐지 마음을 파고드는 한마디, 일생 동안 잊을 수 없는 구절, 상대에게 호감을 주거나 실망을 안겨주는 대화 등이 있지요. 또한 감정적인 표현은 문법이 전혀 맞지 않는 경우도 있습니다.

처음 외국어를 배울 때는 누구나 언어의 신비한 힘에 매료됩니다. 그러나 안타깝게도 문법의 소용돌이에 휘말리면서 어느새 언어에 신비한 힘이 있다는 사실조차 까맣게 잊어버리고 맙니다. 모든 문장을 문법적으로만 이해하려 들고 언어의 신비한 힘은 착각에 불과하지 않을까 하고 생각하게도 됩니다. 하지만 언어에는 분명히 문법이나 논리만으로는 설명할 수 없는 신비한 힘이 있습니다.

학교에서 배우는 '영어' 과목에 질려버려서 이제 영어라면 자신이 없는 분들은 반드시 언어의 본질적인 측면을 다시 살펴보길 바랍니다. 그러면 처음으로 외국어를 접했을 때 느꼈던 그 신비한 느낌이 되살아날 겁니다. 그리고 문법은 서툴지언정 마음이 담긴 '나의 외국어도 통할 수 있다'는 믿음이 다시 우러나올 것입니다.

일반 영어, 변형된 영어, 어려운 영어, 서툰 영어, 단어 수가 제한된 영어, 문법이 파괴된 영어, 거친 영어, 처음 들어보는 영어…….

전부 다 영어입니다. 교과서에 실린 영어는 그 중 하나에 불과합니다. 교과서에 실린 영어만이 '바른 영어'가 아닙니다. 그러므로 자신의 영어는 자신만이 구사할 수 있다는 자신감을 가지고 사용했으면 합니다.

그러면 영어도 신비한 힘을 반드시 발휘하기 시작할 것입니다.

이 시리즈는 영문법 교재가 아닙니다. 학습서도 아닙니다. '영어 읽기'를 최우선 목표로 삼고 쓴 책입니다. 몸으로 체험하고 느낄 수 있도록 기존 영문법과는 조금 다른 해석을 실은 부분도 있습니다. 어디까지나 이제 막 영어 읽기를 시작하는 학생들의 이해를 돕기 위해서 의도적으로 도입한 장치들입니다.

STAFF

written and produced by Takahiko Mukoyama	기획 · 원작 · 글 · 해설 무코야마 다카히코
illustrated by Tetsuo Takashima	그림 · 캐릭터 디자인 다카시마 데츠오
translated by Eun Ha Kim	우리말 번역 김은하
art direction by Yoji Takemura	아트 디렉터 다케무라 요지
technical advice by Fumika Nagano	테크니컬 어드바이저 나가노 후미카
edited by Will Books Editorial Department	편집 윌북 편집부
English-language editing by Michael Keezing	영문 교정 마이클 키징
supportive design by Will Books Design Department	디자인 협력 윌북 디자인팀
supervised by Atsuko Mukoyama Yoshihiko Mukoyama	감수 무코야마 아츠코(梅光学院大学) 무코야마 요시히코(梅光学院大学)
a studio ET CETERA production	제작 스튜디오 엣세트러
published by Will Books Publishing Co.	발행 윌북

special thanks to:

Mac & Jessie Gorham
Baiko Gakuin University

series dedicated to "Fuwa-chan", our one and only special cat

Studio ET CETERA는 야마구치현 시모노세키시에서 중학교 시절을 함께 보낸 죽마고우들이 의기투합하여 만든 기획 집단입니다. 우리 스튜디오는 작가, 프로듀서, 디자이너, 웹마스터 등 다재다능한 멤버들로 구성되어 있으며 주로 출판 분야에서 엔터테인먼트와 감성이 결합된 작품을 만드는 것을 목표로 하고 있습니다.
ET CETERA라는 이름은 어떤 분류에도 속할 수 있으면서 동시에 어떤 분류에도 온전히 속하지 않는 '그 외'라는 뜻의 et cetera에서 따왔습니다. 우리들만이 할 수 있는 독특한 작품을 만들겠다는 의지의 표현이자 '그 외'에 속하는 많은 사람들을 위해 작품을 만들겠다는 소망이 담긴 이름입니다.

옮긴이 **김은하**

유년 시절을 일본에서 보낸 추억을 잊지 못해 한양대학교에서 일어일문학을 전공했다. 어려서부터 한일 양국의 언어를 익힌 덕분에 번역이 천직이 되었다. 번역하는 틈틈이 바른번역 글밥 아카데미에서 출판 번역 강의를 겸하고 있다. 주요 역서로 〈클래식, 나의 뇌를 깨우다〉, 〈지구 온난화 충격 리포트〉, 〈세계에서 제일 간단한 영어책〉, 〈빅팻캣의 영어 수업: 영어는 안 외우는 것이다〉 등 다수가 있다.

Big Fat Cat vs. Mr. Jones
빅팻캣과 미스터 존스 빅팻캣 시리즈 5

펴낸날 개정판 1쇄 2018년 5월 20일
  개정판 5쇄 2024년 5월 24일
글작가 무코야마 다카히코
그림작가 다카시마 데츠오
옮긴이 김은하

펴낸이 이주애, 홍영완
펴낸곳 (주)윌북
출판등록 제2006-000017호

주소 10881 경기도 파주시 광인사길 217
전자우편 willbooks@naver.com
전화 031-955-3777
팩스 031-955-3778
홈페이지 willbookspub.com
블로그 blog.naver.com/willbooks 포스트 post.naver.com/willbooks
트위터 @onwillbooks 인스타그램 @willbooks_pub

ISBN 979-11-5581-169-6 14740